Praise for

The Owner's Manual to Life

"Michael Zajaczkowski's *The Owner's Manual to Life* is a warm, profound, and delightful read. With wit and wisdom, it more than fills the gaps in our education, offering invaluable guidance for those seeking to live their best life."

—Julie Matheson, MA, RScP, author of *Lotus Flower Living: A Journaling Practice for Deep Discovery and Lasting Peace— Untangle Your Mind and Heart Once and for All*

"Simple and clear, heartfelt and incisive, *The Owner's Manual to Life,* is the guidebook we all should have read when we were growing up. Michael Zajaczkowski has pulled together some of the best thoughts around navigating the complexities of life. Read it through once and then read it daily."

—Jerry Colonna, author of *Reboot: Leadership and the Art of Growing Up* and *Reunion: Leadership and the Longing to Belong*

"In *The Owner's Manual to Life*, Michael Zajaczkowski has compiled 100 of the most important life lessons, and in his unique way makes them accessible and exciting for everyone. This book will truly make you worry less and enjoy life more!"

—Brian Tracy, author/speaker/consultant

"I've been a mega-fan of Michael Z's for years now, and his latest manuscript does not disappoint. A delicious blend of insightful, practical, and most of all, gentle suggestions for handling life more gracefully. This meaningful book will leave a lasting impact, and I suspect you'll return to it again and again for its wisdom, compassion, and for its useful lessons. I highly recommend you keep it close for regular doses of inspiration."

—**Katherine Woodward Thomas,** *New York Times*
bestselling author of *Calling in "The One:"*
7 Weeks to Attract the Love of Your Life

"Michael Z's message is rooted in gratitude and curiosity, reminding us that practicing deep acceptance takes attention, reflection, and resilience. He invites readers to reflect through the gracious and tender lens of understanding within their own experience."

—**Sharon Salzberg,** author of *Lovingkindness* and *Real Life*

"Imagine sitting across from your favorite teacher and asking for their advice on how to live your best life. Their answers—as shared through Michael Zajaczkowski's stories, lessons, and insights—are in this humorous, delightful, and inspiring collection of essays. *The Owner's Manual to Life* is about to become your most dog-eared guidebook."

—**Kathleen Guthrie Woods,** creator of 52Nudges
and author of *The Mother of All Dilemmas*

The Owner's Manual to Life In case you missed that day in school when they handed it out...

SIMPLE STRATEGIES
TO WORRY LESS AND
ENJOY LIFE MORE

MICHAEL ZAJACZKOWSKI

Health Communications, Inc.
Boca Raton, Florida

www.hcibooks.com

Library of Congress Cataloging-in-Publication Data
is available through the Library of Congress

© 2023 Michael Zajaczkowski

ISBN-13: 978-07573-2476-5 (Paperback)
ISBN-10: 07573-2476-2 (Paperback)
ISBN-13: 978-07573-2477-2 (ePub)
ISBN-10: 07573-2477-0 (ePub)

Publisher: Health Communications, Inc.
        301 Crawford Boulevard, Suite 200
        Boca Raton, FL 33432–3762

Cover, interior design, and typesetting by Larissa Hise Henoch
Author photo © Carina Gonzalez

To my darling wife, Qi.
I am a better man, in
every way, because of you.

Contents

62. Anger is one letter away from danger. • 173

63. You can always start your day over. • 175

64. How to overcome a resentment. • 177

65. Don't ruin an apology with an excuse. • 179

66. Choose whom you spend time with. • 183

67. "The surest sign of wisdom is constant cheerfulness." —Michel de Montaigne • 187

68. Seek ways to be of service. • 189

69. You don't know what you don't know. • 191

70. Share a memory with someone you love. • 195

71. "Think in the morning. Act in the noon. Eat in the evening. Sleep in the night." —William Blake • 197

72. It is what it is, but it will become what you make it. • 199

73. The difference between heaven and hell. • 201

74. Become willing. • 203

75. Feed your mind as carefully as you feed your stomach. • 205

Acknowledgments

Writing seems to be a solitary process. As writers, we develop an idea for a book, begin crafting that idea into sentences and paragraphs, and finally produce what we believe to be the finished manuscript. What we come to discover, however, is that it is only through the dedication and caring help of others that the work becomes the polished vision we had for it from the beginning.

I am grateful to many people who devoted countless hours to make this manuscript the book you hold in your hands today. To start with, I'd like to thank my wife, Qi Han, with whom I discussed innumerable ideas and quotes, and who made gentle and loving suggestions that gave me the inspiration I needed to say what I truly meant. Thank you, darling Qi, for always being willing to patiently read it just one more time. Next, I'd like to thank my sister-in-law, Laurei Brooks, who read a few of the early quotes and gave me important feedback that helped me position myself properly within the material and allowed me to give it the clarity and honesty I intended.

I am also grateful for the readers and editors who helped guide the writing to where it needed to go. First, thank you, Linda Maynard, for being so willing to read my initial draft, for coming over to my home to pick up the manuscript, and for bringing it back to me with your helpful and insightful comments. I have benefited from your editorial help twice now, and your crucial direction and intuition on my other book was lifesaving. Thank you! And thank you, Bridget Fogarty, for taking the time to carefully read the final manuscript and for not only catching the things I missed but for also pointing out those passages that were either unclear or that needed better or different examples. Your willingness to get involved with this book has made it so much better.

And a special thanks goes out to Shauna Vick, who, from the very beginning, dived in and became the editor I didn't even know I needed. Shauna, your diligent and discerning work, the hours you put into the manuscript, despite all your other responsibilities, and your line-by-line comments, suggestions, and changes transformed my initial manuscript into the polished book it is today. Thank you for challenging me and for encouraging me to own it and to write the best book I was capable of.

I would also like to thank the many people I have met, worked with, and who allowed me to be a part of their lives over the years. You have all taught me much about life and how to live it honestly, with compassion and understanding. I am also indebted to the various people whose quotes I gained so much wisdom from and from whom I gathered so many valuable insights. I endeavored to give full and proper credit where due, and any mistakes in attribution lie solely with me; I apologize in advance for any errors.

Finally, I'd like to thank the diligent and creative team at Health Communications, Inc. (HCI), including Larissa Henoch, who designed such a stunning cover and willingly turned out several versions to help get it just right; the careful copyeditors and proof-readers whose attention to detail helped us turn out the best manu-script possible; and everyone else who invested so much and lent a loving hand to produce such a beautiful book. And a special thanks to Christine Belleris, who championed this book from the very be-ginning, carefully proofread and made invaluable suggestions, and who had the faith to make it an HCI title. I am grateful to you all.

Introduction

We either make ourselves miserable, or we make ourselves strong. The amount of work is the same.
—Carlos Castaneda

Have you ever noticed how some people handle life more gracefully than others? How they seem to be more easygoing, are quick to smile and laugh, and how they're able to worry less and enjoy life more? Whenever the inevitable problem or situation comes up in their lives, they become more composed; they take their time and think about their options, talk to others who have had similar problems, and, when they're ready, they try the first solution. If that doesn't work, they have a backup plan or two in place, and they calmly go about trying another until it works. It's as if they intuitively know how to handle things, as if they had a chip installed that came with an encyclopedia of all possible scenarios, along with various answers and solutions, and they seem to possess the patience and presence of mind to try them. They also seem to know how to appreciate the things around them more. They appear more centered; they smile often and don't take things too seriously. If we used a word to describe them, we'd say they were happy and that they knew peace and contentment. It's as though they were given an owner's manual to life a long time ago, and they studied it carefully.

And have you ever noticed other people who treat life's problems as if they were one emergency after another? Instead of coping mechanisms and problem-solving skills, these people default to states of worry or fearing the worst or self-defeating self-talk like "Why me?" or "Why does something always have to go wrong?" It's as if a lifetime of experiencing problems has conditioned them to imagine that a black cloud follows them, and them only, and that any chance at peace or contentment is slim, if possible at all. Moreover, rather than learning from the last problem or situation, each time a new one comes up, as they always do, it starts a familiar cascade of negative thinking that doesn't encourage solution finding and robs them of the calm they need to maintain the right perspective and find some peace and even humor as they move through their daily life. It's as if they missed that day in school when the teacher handed out the instruction manual to life and with that, they missed the strategies they needed to live life with more peace, joy, and contentment.

In reality, many of us fall somewhere between the two extremes above, though if we admit it, we probably spend more time in the second group than we'd like. The good news is that since we have all experienced those times when we did learn and leverage some experience from the past, when we did solve a problem without letting it drive us crazy, it means that we do have the capacity for better problem-solving, and perhaps all we need is a bit more instruction and some examples that can help us. And that's where this guide comes in handy.

The Owner's Manual to Life is the missing manual many of us haven't had access to before. It's the book of problem-solving that those with the most grace and patience use regularly and have memorized to help them through the occasional storm that blows by, or for the seemingly constant minor annoyances and problems we all face. Inside, you'll find one hundred tips, strategies, and proven ways of responding to life that will instantly give you the toolkit you'll need to both adjust your perspective and handle problems and situations the way you've always wanted to. Once you learn these solutions and begin trying them in your life, what you'll find is that you'll no longer dread problems or be thrown out of whack emotionally; rather, you'll accept them for what they are: simply a natural part of living. Moreover, you'll see them for what they can be: opportunities to learn and grow and become wiser. And the wiser you are, the more you'll be able to relax and let go of things that might be making you unhappy. In addition, *The Owner's Manual to Life* is also filled with tips to help you truly enjoy life more, to remind you to stop and smell the roses, and to take in the immense beauty and joy that we tend to overlook or take for granted.

Writing this book has been a transformative experience for me. While I've been using these techniques for years, by collecting them all in one place and revisiting their usefulness in my life and in the lives of others, I've rediscovered their worth and the wisdom they hold. Midway through the writing of this book, I began observing my tendencies when out in public, and it's taught me, once again, to be more patient and much kinder toward others and to be grateful for what I have.

I was at a matinee movie the other day with my wife, for example, and there was an older couple at the concession stand in front of us. They were in their eighties, and the husband, who was using a walker, ordered and moved at a glacial pace. We had arrived late, and my first impulse was to try to hurry them along, or at the very least cast an impatient stare their way. But I remembered the quote I had just written that day, "Be kind, everyone you meet is fighting a great battle," the one about practicing patience and understanding. In that moment, I was able to rein in my hurried tendency and instead shift my attention to having empathy for what others are going through. As I did, I observed what a tremendous struggle it was for them to just order a popcorn, soda, and nachos and how difficult it was for them to carry these into the movie theater (he was experienced with this as he set them all on the seat of his walker and slowly steered them into the theater).

By just taking a couple of deep breaths, I slowed down and got to a place of gratitude for my own life. I looked at my naturally patient wife, and she smiled up at me, and in that moment, I shifted my attention, and a new appreciation washed over me. Here I was, in the middle of a Tuesday afternoon, at a movie with my wife, a true luxury in itself. And, of course, we had plenty of time to catch the final trailer and start enjoying our popcorn and sodas. I thought about that brief experience, and I realized that, yet again, the wisdom in these simple strategies is always available to me, and they will always make my life better when I remember to use them.

This is what I hope you receive from this book: new tools and tips to live your life with less stress, and instead, to live it more gracefully, more mindfully, with an increased awareness of and appreciation for the joy that is available to you whenever you slow down to see it. I also hope the wisdom in this book inspires you to do more than just read it; I hope it encourages you to interact with it, to dog-ear your favorite passages or highlight quotes in the table of contents so you can return to them again and again. I resisted the urge to categorize the material because I wanted the book to be new and fresh each time you open it. That way, a forgotten passage might speak to you and offer you the tip or strategy just when you need it most.

Life truly is rich and full of wondrous presents, and, as one of the sayings reminds us, it's up to us to untie the ribbons of these gifts each day. Having this owner's manual with you as you go through life's journey will help smooth out the bumps in the road you encounter, and, hopefully, the peaks and valleys you may experience now will soon become gentle rolling hills instead.

Is that a bad thing?

When things don't go our way, or when something happens that we consider to be a bad thing, we can sometimes become annoyed or upset. Once time has passed and we have the benefit of perspective, however, we often find out later that it wasn't such a bad thing after all.

Once, while working as a consultant out of my home office, the Internet went out right in the middle of a huge project. I thought it was the end of the world rather than just an annoyance, and I worried and stressed myself silly, spent hours finding a new router, and then waited impatiently for an IT guy to install it. When all was said and done, however, I found something I hadn't expected: I now had much better Internet coverage throughout my entire house!

Later that night, my wife and I processed this experience, and we realized that what at first seemed to be a disaster turned out to be a blessing in disguise. My wife looked at me and said, "Maybe having the Internet go out wasn't such a bad thing after all." From that experience, we came up with a saying we now use whenever something unexpected, or what we used to consider bad, comes up. We simply look at the situation and ask ourselves, "Is that a bad thing?"

Meeting so-called problems or situations with this new awareness and attitude will transform your life. Now, when something breaks, goes out, or doesn't go the way we planned (and it could be a small thing like the faucet leaking or a bigger thing like a vacation being canceled), we instantly ask, "Is that a bad thing?" Then we shift our attention and begin looking for the ways the situation can be improved, or search for new opportunities that might be even better for us. When we do, we often find better upgrades for what we had, or newer, improved ways of doing what we had planned.

After doing this now for years, we've discovered that just because something doesn't go the way we thought it should, it doesn't mean that it didn't go the best way it could. Everyone has experiences like this, and I'm sure you can think back to earlier disappointments that, in the end, turned out to be a good thing as well. By adopting this new attitude, you will discover a much better way of dealing with the inevitable changes life presents you with. By developing the habit of asking, "Is that a bad thing?" you'll be able to see past the obstacles that used to frustrate you and make you unhappy. Plus, you'll now be on the lookout for better ways to improve your life—and your life experience.

Stop comparing and judging; start identifying and connecting.

L et's face it, people are different. They'll do things you won't agree with, hold certain beliefs that will be the complete opposite to what you believe, and they'll act in ways that, at times, might seem deliberately hurtful, disrespectful, or just plain nuts. People are people, which means they have limitations, and sometimes we all scratch our heads over their decisions, actions, or attitudes. By the way, this includes your family members, your kids, spouse, and even yourself on occasion.

Whenever I'm faced with a difficult person, or when someone is acting in a way I don't approve of, I always remember the Native American proverb that says, "Never judge another man until you've walked a mile in his moccasins." What this reminds me of is that I have no idea of the challenges this person has had to deal with in their life. I have no idea of their upbringing, or the prejudice they may have been taught or experienced as a child. I know nothing of their education—or lack of education—nor of the life pressures they may be under. Who knows, given what they've had to overcome, I could be much worse if I were dealt the same circumstances. They may be doing remarkably well, all things considered.

Once I think about these things, really take them in, and weigh them against what I don't know about someone, I begin to move past my own judgment. And this allows me to start identifying. It doesn't take much self-searching to realize there have been times when I've acted in a similar way to what I may be objecting to right now. Certainly, if I don't agree with a person's opinion, that means I feel just as strongly about an opposite point of view, and to that person, I may be considered just as wrong as I think they are. Same thing with actions I may find rude or insensitive. For example, whenever I see someone throw a cigarette out of a car window, my first reaction is to judge, "Oh, how disrespectful that is!" Then I remind myself that when I was smoking many years ago, I undoubtedly did the same thing and never gave it a second thought.

Once I start looking for ways to identify with someone, or make an attempt to understand the circumstances that shaped them, I begin looking for the similarities between us. We all have a need for security and health, and we all carry love in our hearts for our families and look after them the best we know how. Most people pursue a spiritual or religious path and have the same questions I do about our purpose and the meaning of life. As I look for what's the same in others, it makes it easier to get to know them, to engage with them, and to even learn from them. This willingness to identify is the beginning of true compassion.

As I get to the place of acceptance of another person, state, or even country, I begin searching for the connection between us, and I see the truth in our common experience: while we may all wear different moccasins, we're all walking a similar path called life. And in this life, the journey is much easier for us all if we strive to identify and concentrate on how we're the same rather than how we're different.

"You grow up the day you have your first real laugh at yourself."

—Ethel Barrymore

Many of us take life very seriously. We're constantly on guard to present our best selves to people, and we're deathly afraid of looking bad or not having the right answers. As children, our parents teach us to dress and act right and to have proper manners. As we become teenagers, the need to be cool and part of the in-crowd is painfully important to us. It doesn't get easier in college, either. Suddenly, the competition for attention, for grades, and for looking better than everyone else increases. After graduation, when we enter the job market, and as we begin seriously dating and trying to find the right spouse, we continue to compare and compete. There is tremendous pressure on us to grow up and become adults, and it can take a long time to learn how to be comfortable just being ourselves.

I remember the first time I had a good laugh at myself. While eating out with a group of people, I struggled to open a ketchup bottle, and someone close to me pointed out that I had made a mess of my shirt and hadn't noticed. As the group began giggling at me, I felt my cheeks flush with embarrassment. As I glanced down at the sauce splattered on my white shirt, it suddenly occurred to me that it *was* pretty funny. Hilarious, even. When I looked back up at the group of people trying to contain their amusement and cover their smiles, I instantly felt the urge to laugh along with them, so I did. Once they saw I wasn't taking offense at them enjoying the scene I'd made, they laughed even more, and soon, tears were running down my cheeks—that's how hard I was laughing! I'm smiling even now as I remember this. In that moment, I had the first real laugh at myself, and I felt the relief of years of trying to look good melt away. I felt a freedom I hadn't experienced before; I guess that is what growing up feels like!

What it comes down to is not taking yourself too seriously. Once you have that first good laugh at yourself, and then many more later, you realize that life is best worn as a loose garment. Things really aren't as serious as we think they are, and everyone makes mistakes—more than we'd like to admit. No one is perfect, and one of my favorite expressions is "Even monkeys fall out of trees." Once you release yourself from trying to look perfect all the time, you give yourself more room to experiment, more permission to try new things, and the freedom to just be you. When you learn to laugh at yourself and take things less seriously, other people become more attracted to you as well. They, too, will feel comfortable being themselves around you, and they'll be able to relate to you more. Remember: we're all in this together, just doing the best we can. Sometimes, that's pretty funny to watch.

Trying to meditate is the same thing as meditating.

Meditation is an invaluable tool to deepen our spiritual practices, as well as reduce stress and become more centered, and as a way of developing mindfulness and living more in the present. Those who have developed a regular practice often say that meditation is as important in their daily lives as eating or sleeping. If you have tried meditating, then you may have glimpsed the peaceful feelings you get as the world slows down and you learn to let go. Yet again, you may also have experienced how difficult it is to get your mind to stay in one place for even a few seconds.

Ping! Another text has arrived. As you grab your phone to see who it is, you notice you also have three new emails. As you swipe to see who they're from, you see alerts of new posts on your social media feeds or updates on breaking news stories. This is just the activity on your phone! Our minds have been conditioned to multitask, to always be on the go, so retraining them to be still, focused, quiet—even for a few minutes—seems like an impossible task. Thankfully, just *attempting* to slow down and meditate, regardless of whether you think you're successful at it, is the same as actually doing it, and it will give you the same benefits.

A spiritual teacher I worked with years ago explained it to me this way: he asked if I decided to take up tennis, invested in a racket, learned the rules, and then played regularly, would I consider myself a tennis player? I suppose, I said, but not a very good one. But, he said, *you're still playing tennis, right*? I admitted I was. He told me it's the same with meditating. If I developed a regular time to get quiet, showed up each day, set my timer, and started counting my breaths and watching my thoughts glide by, then I'd be meditating. Like playing tennis, some days I'd do better than others, yet overall, I'd still benefit from doing it regularly.

Explained in this way, I was able to let go of my expectations and judgments about *how* I was doing it, and I just started doing it. Each morning, I'd show up and sit as still as I could and begin counting my breaths. If I lost count, I'd simply go back to one and start over. Some days, ten minutes would fly by, while other days, two minutes seemed like twenty, and it was difficult to keep my mind from jumping all over the place. Even though I wasn't doing it perfectly, I realized that I was indeed meditating. I found that each quiet period I spent trying to meditate changed me for the better. Life seemed less urgent; I became more present and was even able to appreciate some of the small moments of magic that are in each day.

If you've wondered about meditating, or even tried it a few times and failed at it, I urge you to try again. Just the act of sitting down and attempting to watch your thoughts enter and leave your head, while you count your breaths and slow down, will help you develop some space, and a sense of peace will enter your life. Just remember: the moment you try to do something, you're doing it. If you keep at it, the benefits will always follow.

5

"Happiness is pretty simple— someone to love, something to do, something to look forward to."

—Rita Mae Brown

This is one of my favorite quotes because of its simplicity and the depth of its wisdom. *Someone to love* reminds me that I am happiest when I have someone else to think about and to care for. In addition to the powerful gift love gives us both, the reason this allows me to feel happiness is that when I'm focused on others, I'm not thinking about myself. And the less I'm thinking about myself—my problems, or the things I don't have or won't get, etc., the more peace and contentment I have.

The second part—*something to do*—reminds me of a quote by Mark Twain: "To be busy is man's only happiness." I don't know about you, but if I wake up on a Saturday with a list of activities or a plan for the day, I wake up energized with a purpose. On the other hand, if I have nothing to do, I tend to be lethargic, unfocused, and my mind tends to find things to worry about. It's like what works with kids: structure always provides security and comfort. Every day, I make sure I have a plan—or at least options—even if that plan is to read and nap on the couch in the afternoon.

This leads to the third part—*something to look forward to*. Whether it's the weekend, your next vacation, or your kid's school play, having something to look forward to helps give meaning and payoff to the work and responsibilities we all have. This is why I always have a trip (even if it's just a three-day weekend) planned and placed in the calendar. I think about it and look forward to the break. My wife and I talk about and enjoy planning it weeks in advance. Something to look forward to breaks up the monotony our daily grind can become and makes life enjoyable and worthwhile.

So, if you're not feeling happy or motivated these days, just review this simple recipe for happiness. Consider what you can add or change in your life. Any of these three ingredients will make an immediate impact on your level of happiness and contentment.

6

Remember: success is a journey, not a destination.

It is a common experience to look back fondly to our college days. The comradery, the student lounges, the quads, the football games in the fall, and so much more. We also remember how we couldn't wait for finals to be over, to graduate and finally begin real life, to get our first job and start climbing the ladder of success. Success that was once defined by getting that college diploma, however, was quickly replaced with getting that promotion or that new home or marrying him or her and having kids, and so on. Now that some of us are much further down the road of life, we look back wistfully to those innocent years in college, those carefree days (or so they seem now), and wish we could wander down to the student center one more time and order a latte and then curl up with the classic book assigned in our English lit class. Oh, the good old days . . .

I could paint the same scenario about my professional career: entering as an intern, going independent and establishing my own business, longing, struggling, wishing to be successful already. We can apply this "wanting to reach our destination" to many other situations in our lives, big and small: having kids, waiting for them to grow up or grow out of "that phase," move out, establish their own path, get married, and so on. On a smaller scale, we can't wait for that upcoming vacation, then to the next country or hotel, then home and onto planning the next one. But in our drive to reach the various destinations in life, sure that once we finally achieve this or that we'll be happy or acknowledged or free, we often find the *next* destination tempting us, promising us that this will be the one to complete us. Accomplish this, it seems to say, and you will have finally arrived. Though we all know the truth, don't we?

The hardest thing, it seems, is to learn to enjoy the journey. As the train of life barrels down the tracks, too few of us remember to look out and enjoy the passing scenery. We fail to look around the carriage and visit with our fellow passengers; we neglect the precious moments we spend in the car, fail to feel the binding of the books in our laps. These little things, however, are what make up the journey of life, the journey toward the success that we mistake as the destination. True success is learning to get present and appreciate the moments, the interactions, the small joys that make up the fabric of our lives. Rather than keeping our eyes on the end of the journey, it's by enjoying where our feet are right now that gives everything we're going through meaning and purpose.

As you read this quote today, take a moment to think about where you are in your own journey through life. How old are you? What part of this amazing world do you live in? What season is it? What are you eating or drinking right now? Who do you love, and who loves you? You see, regardless of the various destinations you're trying to get to, nothing is as precious as the time you're spending right now, and all the joy, peace, sense of accomplishment you seek, you already have access to right now; you simply need to stop and recognize it. When you do, you'll understand that success truly does lie in the journey, the wonderful journey of life, and the journey you're on right now, right here. By learning to enjoy this very moment, you'll have arrived at your destination.

7

"Life is half delicious yogurt, half crap, and your job is to keep the plastic spoon in the yogurt."

—Scott Adams

This saying reminds me of an important truth, and one I tend to forget: where I place my attention determines my mood, influences my attitudes, and affects my relationships with other people. It also reminds me that in life, there are both wondrous and beautiful things, like stunning sunsets, the light in a child's eye, the touch from a loved one, as well as darker things like cruelty, bigotry, and suffering. Most of all, it reminds me that I have a choice as to where I keep my plastic spoon.

The way to stay focused on the delicious yogurt is to maintain an attitude of gratitude. You can do this by either mentally counting all the things you're grateful for or by making a written list of the things you have and enjoy in your life. It's best to start with the things most of us have that we take for granted yet are truly miraculous: the ability to see and hear and appreciate those beautiful sunsets, for example. Next, most of us have loving families and friends who add so much meaning to our lives. To feel heard and understood and loved for who you are is a precious gift indeed. When you consider the quality of life you can access in the twenty-first century, including advanced medical care, abundant material items including cars, tech devices, the Internet (an endless list, really), you realize that you have it better than generations of people who came before you. We are truly blessed.

On the other hand, life can seem pretty crappy, too. Just because we have access to so much, it's also easy to think of all the things we don't have. If we don't have a car, we want one, or a better one, or a better house, a better spouse, etc. Watch the news: there is abundant evidence of injustice, suffering, and bad people doing evil things and getting away with it. We are bombarded by all the crap in the world, and it's far too easy to go negative by moving our spoon into it, and as soon as we do, we become cranky, irritable, and even depressed. This quote teaches us to remember that we have a job to do: to keep our spoon in the delicious yogurt. When we remember we have this choice—and we exercise it—then we're able to appreciate the deliciousness of our lives and give gratitude for all the wonderful things in it.

8

Focus on the twenty-four hours ahead of you.

Have you ever had one of those mornings where you've woken up tired from all the things you were thinking about the night before? Then, as you lie there in bed, you begin adding to that list all the things you've got to do that day, and tomorrow, and all the things that have to go right that week and month, and then you find yourself six months down the line, worrying and plotting and trying to anticipate outcomes and planning reactions and on and on? When that happens, we exhaust ourselves before we've even brushed our teeth. And that's just the first fifteen minutes of the day!

It's easy to get overwhelmed when we try to tackle too much at once, and it rarely helps because things are constantly changing, and variables we can't control, let alone anticipate, always pop up—for good and for bad. Rather than waste precious energy and imagination on a future you can't predict, a better strategy is to focus on the more immediate present, breaking it down to just the next twenty-four hours at a time.

The moment I bring myself back to today, I find that my life instantly becomes manageable again. As soon as I shed the future, I easily identify the actions (and thoughts) I can take today that will allow me to feel in control again—thus relieving me of much anxiety and fear—and that helps to restore a sense of calm. It is from a calm

21

place that I inevitably make better decisions, and I also choose steps that will move me closer to the future I want.

An example is when I used to worry endlessly about being self-employed. Would I find enough clients to be successful? Would I earn enough money this month to cover my expenses? What if I don't make it over the next six months? Will I be able to get a regular job? Would I be all right with working for someone else? I could torture myself with these and other thoughts until I was exhausted before breakfast. More importantly, none of these thoughts or worries of the future helped me.

What did help was when I focused on my plans and actions in the next twenty-four hours. Suddenly, I could take definite actions today that would advance my goals, that would lead to making money and building my business, and that would, if I stayed focused on them, make that day a success. What I hoped would happen did: successful twenty-four-hour days turned into successful months and quarters. My progress sometimes looked like a stock chart, with peaks and valleys; however, the overall trajectory was positive. And it all started by concentrating on today.

They say a journey of a thousand miles begins with a single step. I'd say that to accomplish that journey, it's a lot easier focusing on the steps you can take today—instead of planning a thousand steps out. We all have twenty-four hours, and if we do our best with those hours, and stay present within them, then we can all accomplish any journey, and we will be sane, centered, and even happy as we do.

9

If you don't like someone, get to know them better.

Have you ever met someone who instantly annoyed you? Sometimes, it's just incompatibility between the two of you, but in other cases you discover that other people feel the same way about that person. He or she doesn't seem to have many friends, and they don't get invited to many group gatherings. The person might be unpleasant or downright rude and contentious. It could be a coworker, a neighbor, or an acquaintance who we run into at regular functions. Like others, we usually avoid these people, turn the other way when we see them, or find an excuse to talk to someone else or move to a different room. What we may suspect—and most certainly is happening—is the other person feels our avoidance, and this undoubtably alienates them further. I once learned a better way of dealing with difficult people, and each time I'm willing to try it, I'm always surprised by what I learn.

Years ago, I played a lot of tennis at the local park. Many of the same players showed up each week, and we all got to know one another. One day, a new player showed up. He had a very aggressive style of play, and he wasn't as good as the rest of us regulars. I dreaded having to play with him, as I felt I was so much better and that my level of play would suffer by playing down to his level. When we played our first game, he beat me! We played again, and he beat me again! Then, each time I saw him, he smirked at me, and I grew angry and more frustrated. After weeks of seeing him, other players avoided being paired with him, and over and over it was left to me to be his partner. I complained to a friend of mine about this guy, and my friend made the oddest suggestion: Why don't you get to know him better?

While I thought this was the silliest thing I'd ever heard, I decided to try it. I began by purposefully asking to play with him and then spent time between matches talking with him, getting to know him. We exchanged phone numbers, and he began calling to set up practice sessions. I found him to be very reliable, dedicated, and after getting to know him better, I discovered that beneath that rough and aggressive exterior, he was really a sweet guy. As he opened up to me, I learned his dad was not in a good way, and his mother had her hands full caring for him. His parents lived in the next state, and he spent a lot of time driving there to help out. His burden at the time was heavy, and his release was tennis, but no one at the park was willing to look beyond his gruff personality, which only made him feel more left out. He went on to become a consistent player and someone I could depend on for a lot more than just tennis, and we became friends.

I suspect we all know someone like this, and some of you have taken time to befriend them and learned that beneath a hard exterior often lives a softer, kinder person. Often, it seems as though people who push others away want and need the same kind of connection we're all looking for; it just doesn't come easy for them. Not everyone we try to befriend turns out to be someone we want to hang out with long term, and that's as it should be. If we're willing to at least extend ourselves, get to know someone, and give them the kindness we would like ourselves, then we'll inevitably find that they want the same things we do: acceptance, companionship, and a chance to belong. So, the next time you're faced with someone you don't like, get to know them better. You might both be happy you did.

10

"Never hurry, and never worry."

—E. B. White

When I first read this quote, I felt as though I was finally given permission to reverse the way I'd gone through much of my life. Even as a child, I'd had a lot to worry about: my parents' divorce, separating from my siblings, moving around the country in the middle of each school year while my mom and stepdad searched for better jobs or a new start, and more. I learned to worry about things and rush through my young life, trying to stay one step ahead of the next unwelcome change. Many people I work with also feel the need to hurry through things, and worry has become a constant companion for them. E. B. White is the author of some of my favorite childhood books, such as *Charlotte's Web* and *Stuart Little*. His simple saying, "Never hurry, and never worry," allowed me to exhale a big breath of relief, and I was finally able to slow down and get some perspective.

Hurrying rarely gets me ahead of anything; in fact, it usually just frustrates me and those around me. For an example of this, I only have to think of the driver who is in a hurry to pass everyone in front of them. He weaves in and out of traffic, dangerously cutting people off, all in a tremendous hurry—for what? At the next light or freeway exit, I inevitably find myself either behind or beside him. All his hurrying achieved nothing for him—nothing but stress and resentful feelings from other drivers. This is the same for many of us. Hurrying through a task or situation in our lives rarely gives us any additional time. Instead, it robs us of the peace we have access to in every moment. By remembering "to never hurry," I become open to more feelings of calm, and I am able do things much more enjoyably by slowing down and doing them with care and attention.

Discovering the concept of never worrying inspired another revelation as well. I wrote down my current top five worries in my morning journal and then revisited them a month later and recorded what happened with them. My experience showed that each and every one of them ceased being an issue or was resolved despite my fears and worries. Bigger issues sometimes took a little longer, yet they, too, worked out in the end. Writing your worries down helps you put things in perspective and reminds you that "worry is like a rocking chair—it gives you something to do, but it doesn't get you anywhere."

Adopting an attitude of reducing worry and slowing down throughout our days provides us with many benefits. Doing so helps us release stress and reduces the anxiety that can build up during the days or weeks. As we calm down, we become more present, more centered, and more relatable to the people around us. Whenever you find yourself rattled or uncomfortable in a situation, just ask yourself if you're worrying or rushing through something. If so, take a breath or two and remind yourself that all the things you worried about or rushed through in the past all worked out, and that what you're going through right now will, too. So, relax and take it easy.

11

Switch teams on the debate club.

There are always two sides to every story and position. Often, though, we are usually too busy defending our position to stop and consider the other side, but clearly, the other person or group of people believe in their opinion as much as we do ours. In order to understand that other point of view better, both to gain insight into their position and to validate your position more, it's a valuable exercise to switch sides on the debate and argue it from their point of view.

Debate clubs do this all the time and for good reason: there are many insights to be gained by looking at an issue from both sides. By switching sides for a moment, you have the opportunity to fully consider all points of the other side's argument. When you take the time to do this, there might be some things you actually agree with or at least understand better. The deeper you dig into an issue, the more complex it turns out to be, and the more similarities you're likely to find. Another benefit is that you'll come to see the holes or limitations in your own position. After all, there are two sides to every story or issue.

Taking the time to honestly consider another's point of view also increases your capacity to get along with them. Let's face it: we don't all agree on every issue, and that's what diversity is all about. It would be a truly boring world indeed if we all dressed the same, ate the same food, and thought alike. By becoming truly interested in and open to what other people think, why they hold their view, and why it's important to them, you become not only more accepting, you become more tolerant as well. For one thing, you'll come to see that we all want essentially the same things:

- Health for ourselves and our family
- Opportunity for happiness as we define it
- The freedom to pursue what's meaningful to us

I believe that deep down there is a fundamental goodness and desire in all of us to be helpful, and we see this in any disaster situation: people automatically helping each other despite differences of opinion. By focusing on how we're all alike, you increase your capacity for compassion, and you become a gentler, kinder person.

In today's world of differences and increasing divisiveness, switching teams on the debate club can become the bridge back to a more united society and world. While you still might not agree with another person's side of an issue, by being willing to at least understand it better, you'll be quicker to find the areas where your positions are in alignment. At the very least, the other person's attitude might soften when they feel you're taking the time to understand and relate to them. In the end, isn't that what we all want? To be understood and accepted for who we are? This week, pick an issue you feel strongly about, and challenge yourself to debate it from the other side. You might be surprised by what you learn.

12

One sure way to conquer fear: make a decision and take an action.

We all experience fear in our lives—either over an impending event or current situation, or over the consequences of some past situation or decision. Fear is a normal, and even healthy emotion warning us that something is not right and that we need to proceed carefully or reverse or change course. Fear can also help us discover new opportunities and motivate us to make needed changes in our lives. But when fear seizes us, it's sometimes hard to see those opportunities, and if we're not careful, fear can become an obsessive mental habit, both sapping us of strength and draining the joy from our lives.

Often, when we are in fear of something, it is easy to become stuck in and to wallow in that fear. Sometimes we're afraid of how a situation will turn out, and we spend way too much time imagining dark scenarios or painting reactions and outcomes we dread. An example is when something happens to us physically. We find a lump, or some part of our body hurts, or a tooth suddenly becomes sensitive, and we fear the worst. If we stay in this place, fear can build upon itself, and soon we find other things to worry about, and our emotional lives can spiral out of control. The way out of this place is to make a decision and take an action: in this case, to call a doctor and set an appointment. While we may still be afraid, having a plan of action often alleviates our sense of dread and releases us from an unhealthy fear cycle.

Making a decision and taking action also releases us from years of indecision or worry. For a long time, I wanted to go back to school to get a graduate degree in psychology, but I was plagued with fears: Would I get accepted? How would I pay for it? Would I find work afterward? These fears, and others, kept me from taking action until finally one day I made a decision to move forward. That led to my first action: download and fill out the university's application form. In that one moment, years of fear were replaced by feelings of excitement and possibility. I ended up attaining that degree, found a way to pay for it, and I accomplished a lifelong goal. Ultimately, fear will always be a part of our lives. We can either let it control us or decide and act, and so move beyond it. Recognizing you have that choice is the beginning of freedom from fear.

13

Write a heartfelt card to someone you care about.

When was the last time you received an unexpected card in the mail affirming that you are appreciated or loved? Have you ever received one? If you have had this deeply meaningful experience, then you know the special feelings of joy and appreciation that a simple, heartfelt card can bring. While we might experience this once a year on our birthday, it's unfortunate that we have to wait a whole year before we get to feel those warm feelings again.

Today, start a new tradition: Make a list of those people in your life whom you love or care about, those who have shared significant parts of your life or had an impact on you in some meaningful way. Then, write them a short (or longer if the mood strikes you) note, either on nice stationery or in an interesting card, expressing your love, gratitude, or feelings of appreciation. There is something genuine and special about a handwritten note. In this age of instant social media posts, taking the time to sit down and put pen to paper tells the recipient that they mean something to you, and they'll be moved by your thoughtfulness. Imagine the look of surprise and delight on their face when they find a colorful, personalized card from you amid their usual mail of flyers, solicitations, and bills.

Even—or especially—if it has been a long time since you have been in contact, this simple act often leads to a renewed connection, either by phone or maybe even in person, where you can share some memories and feelings of belonging and make some new ones. Sending a heartfelt card helps you both.

You don't have to spend a lot to reap the rewards. When you are out and about, be on the lookout for greeting cards when you're at the market or pharmacy. Browse the dollar store for everyday cards as well as seasonal cards (their Halloween, Thanksgiving, and Christmas cards are nicer than you think). I have found some of the most endearing "Across the miles ..." cards that are perfect for those friends and family members who live far away. By collecting cards in advance like this, it's much easier to act on impulse when you feel the urge to write and send one. I like to keep my cards, along with some fun or inspirational stamps, next to my favorite chair, and I write at least one card a month, and more when I feel the urge to let someone know I'm thinking about them.

Writing a heartfelt card to a distant friend is just the start. There are people in your very household who would not only be surprised to receive a handwritten card from you but who would be touched in a deep way. Did your son or daughter win a big soccer game? Ace a difficult test they studied hard for? How about your spouse? How much would it mean to them to receive an unexpected, handpicked card expressing how much they mean to you? These are the kinds of things our family members will keep and cherish for years. Giving or sending a sincere and unexpected card is a meaningful gesture, and it reminds us that we all have the ability to do one of the most important things in the world: add love and kindness. Nothing you will do today will be more important—or remembered—than that.

Today is the tomorrow you worried about yesterday.

Think back to a year ago. What most worried you? Chances are, you don't remember. Unless it was something monumental, it's likely the troubles and fears you had will have faded or been forgotten. That's the nature of life and something to always remember as you try to maintain your perspective on things. All the todays in which you'll find yourself will come with resolutions and solutions to the problems you worried about yesterday. And the tomorrows you may be dreading right now will eventually become the todays. The key to living with the uncertainties of those approaching tomorrows is to carefully control your energy and direct your focus.

Energy goes where attention flows. What you dwell on expands; what you withdraw from your attention shrinks. If you find yourself obsessing or worrying about a situation, the solution is to withdraw your attention from it. Remove your thoughts from what is, in reality, a temporary state of affairs, and redirect them to either what is happening this very minute or on what's ahead of you today. Chances are, whatever you're worried about isn't happening right now; rather, it is only a possibility in some imagined tomorrow. What's happening today is that you're reading this book. You may be in your living room or office or on a train or at the beach. You may be drinking a cup of tea or eating a snack. Right now, however, the dread attached

to some event in the future, or to scenarios you fear, may not mate-
rialize at all. As Calvin Coolidge once said: "If you see ten troubles
coming down the road, you can be sure that nine will run into the
ditch before they reach you." I know you can relate to this, because it
happens to all of us. By maintaining this perspective of time, and by
remembering our experience of how things work out or don't come
to pass, we begin living more freely, with more peace in today.

The concept of detachment will help you get to this point. Detaching from something doesn't mean you are denying the reality of
it; instead, it means that for the moment, you are simply withdrawing
your energy and attention from it. The situation, fear, or person still
exists, but for this moment or hour or day, you are choosing to detach
from it.

Practicing detachment means you are refusing to be pushed by
the panic you may feel, and you are releasing your attachment to how
things currently appear. By detaching in this way, you cease resisting
the outer picture of events and you refuse to give these passing situations any more of your energy. By withdrawing in this way, you create
the space to place your focus and attention where it belongs: on the
aroma or warmth of the tea you're drinking, and on the awareness
of what is happening today. Detaching is similar to meditating; it's a
skill that requires practice because when our minds are very worried,
they will want to return to the problem. When you notice this, gently
bring your focus back to the now and tell yourself you are detaching
for a moment from the fear or concerns of tomorrow. As you practice
this, you will get better and better at it, and you'll enjoy longer and
longer stretches of time removed from your worries and fears.

It also helps to remind yourself that today is the tomorrow you
worried about yesterday. Doing this reminds you of the impermanence

of time itself, a construct many say that has no real existence other than the definitions we give it. Ultimately, it reminds us that we all live in one eternal "now," in a constant state of today. And today is probably a lot better than what you worried about yesterday.

15

How many psychiatrists does it take to change a lightbulb? Only one—but the lightbulb has to want to change.

This simple joke reveals a lot of wisdom. Therapists are taught to listen, to be patient, to help clients arrive at their own truths. They're taught that until someone is ready to accept that their behavior or thought patterns are no longer working for them, any suggestion or direction the therapist might offer would not only not help them, but if their clients tried it and it didn't work, then they could blame the therapist, and they'd lose a valuable opportunity to help them in the future. This is one reason therapy takes so long to achieve results: people have to arrive at their own solutions and work through their own problems before they're ready to change or try something new.

Most people forget this. Parents are a good example. They have a lot of knowledge and experience, and they sincerely want to help their kids avoid the pain they know certain actions or decisions can bring. They advise their children; they steer them to universities and careers they think are right for them, but in many cases, their kids eventually choose their own paths. It's hard to let go of our need to protect, control, and worry about those we love; however, at some point, we have to acknowledge that we all have our own journey, and it's up to us to take it. If we doubt that, all we have to do is look at our own choices, the lessons we had to learn, and how they formed the person we are today. While we may wish we hadn't gone through some of those experiences, most of us would admit two things: first, no one could have talked us out of doing them at the time, and second, what we learned was invaluable to forming both ourselves and our understanding of the world.

As I sit with friends and family today, I realize the immense wisdom in asking questions and truly listening to people's answers. I know the relative futility of offering suggestions when they aren't asked for. The value I can bring, and that any of us can offer, is to listen and try to understand rather than try to fix someone. It takes tremendous patience, and a lot of love, but until someone asks directly what we think they ought to do or if we have ideas on how to handle something, chances are, they aren't yet ready to climb the ladder and change the lightbulb. This doesn't mean you can't help someone who is struggling with a decision or situation; you can—of course, and you do—by being there for them, by listening and sharing what you did in a similar situation and how that affected you. Ultimately, it may take someone longer than we'd like for them to get to the point of making a change or trying a different path, and that's how it should be. In the end, our only job is to support and love them until they're ready. Just like people loved us.

16

Live life one hour at a time.

L ife happens fast. With kids, work, parents, and a thousand other responsibilities, days, weeks, and whole months can evaporate quickly. The older you get, the faster time flies. *Where did this month or this summer go?* is a question I find myself asking more and more as the days whiz by.

Staying in the moment, in the now, is a lesson many spiritual leaders teach as a way of slowing time down and appreciating the precious gifts each moment holds. Someone once said that each day is the most valuable thing we have, that even if we had all the money in the world, we couldn't purchase one extra hour of this priceless treasure.

There are many ways to practice staying in the now. I've mentioned the strategy of focusing on the twenty-four hours ahead of you, and this is often enough to keep me centered. But sometimes I've just got too much to do, and my mind starts racing, or sometimes things come up that take me out of the day and it's hard to stay in the present; I can find myself lost as the day speeds by and morning blurs into evening.

Living life one hour at a time, however, is the perfect solution. I simply start where I am—it's 9:06 AM right now, for example—and concentrate only on what is happening within this hour; then at 10:06 AM, I ask myself: Where am I? What is the temperature? What colors do I see? Who is with me? What sounds do I hear? What am I grateful for *right now*? By breaking life down this way, I get better and better at not only being more present each hour but also at enjoying those hours more.

I've found this technique both liberating and enriching. Not only does it help ground me and open me up to the gifts of the moment, it's also an effective tool to use if I'm feeling anxious and fearful about some future or past event. If I find myself wandering off into tomorrow or back into yesterday, I simply look at the time and get back to that hour. Best of all, if I find I've strayed too far, I can restart a new hour at any point in the day.

If you're looking for a way to become more peaceful, more centered, and more appreciative of the many gifts you already have, then take an hour and observe all that life presents to you right now. In this very hour. In fact, what time is it?

17

Make a list.

Regularly making lists is a simple yet effective way of staying organized and becoming more efficient. It has other surprising benefits as well. I imagine that many of you make shopping lists or keep track of the kids' activities. If you have a big vacation planned, you might jot down a packing list. It is always easier to write items down on paper (or a note on your phone) when we're thinking of them rather than commit them to memory and try to pull them up down the road when we need them. Anyone who has gone to the market without their grocery list knows how frustrating it is to be back home in the middle of meal preparation and realize that there is one necessary ingredient that you failed to pick up.

Beyond grocery shopping and vacation planning, lists can be helpful in other areas of your life. By learning a few tips, you'll also increase the usefulness of the lists you're already making. One key to improving these lists is to type them up and revise them as things change. I learned this strategy from a good friend who told me she has a travel packing list she prints out whenever she goes on a trip. I've since created my own, and now I have three lists that I update each time I travel. I have a business packing list that includes my work notes, my flash drive, and an iPhone holder for my belt. I also have two vacation lists: one domestic and one international, which includes guidebooks, passport, foreign currency, etc. I also update these lists as things change. If I find I no longer need something—like the bulky, external GPS—I simply delete it and replace it with something new I found I needed on my last trip but forgot to pack. Having a list also helps me to remember those uncommon items I always seem to forget about—like bringing my own pillow for any trips I take by car. The practice of having a reusable list like this makes your life so much easier.

Making a list also helps when you've got a lot on your mind or when you're anxious about something, especially at bedtime. I don't know why my mind likes to pick 10 PM to begin thinking so much, but when it does, I've found it helpful to jot down the issues or potential problems in a small notebook that I keep next to my bed. I know I'll get a better night's rest and therefore be fresh and alert in the morning and better able to come up with the solutions I need. There is something liberating about getting recurring and worrisome thoughts out of my head and onto a written list. When my mind tries to go back over something, I just remind myself that it's safe on the list, and I'll deal with it first thing in the morning. Inevitably, my mind releases the thoughts and quiets itself.

Lists are also an important component to helping you set and achieve goals in your life. One of the strategies I have is to use a notebook to separate out my goals into broad categories: physical, work, creative, spiritual, and so on. I then break down these categories into monthly, quarterly, and yearly mini goals. Each morning, I then create to-do lists for the day that are in alignment with each monthly goal. I find that having a clear direction each morning focuses my time and attention, and I feel much more accomplished by the end of the day when I've checked off the majority of items on each list. Using lists in this way keeps me moving toward longer-term goals by keeping me focused on the things I can do "just for today."

My wife is a big list maker as well, and we often exchange and add to each other's lists. This is a great practice to get into with your family, and doing so will bring you all closer together and keep you all on the same page. We have several notebooks—of different sizes—throughout our home, each for a different project or upcoming event. We find that if we write things down while we're thinking of them, it's easier to transfer to a computer later, thus creating a permanent and reusable list for the next time the same occasion comes up.

I'm sure many of you have your own way of making and using lists. To make them more effective, use some of the ideas you've read about today. If you aren't in the habit of making lists yet, simply grab a couple of notebooks, or even pieces of paper, and place them around your home with a pen next to them. You'll be surprised how much they'll come in handy, and some of you may find yourself wondering how you ever got along without them.

18

If you spot it, you got it!

It's very easy to look at other people and begin counting their flaws. This one has no patience and so gets annoyed and upset quickly. Or maybe a coworker is very ambitious, cutthroat even, and we're put off by their never-ending drive to climb the corporate ladder at everyone else's expense. Parents and siblings are a favorite target because we have lived with their faults and can rattle off every one of them with ease.

This keen ability to spot character flaws happens quickly as well and becomes a sixth sense in a way. Interacting with cashiers at markets, or other people in public, or even over the phone with customer service reps, we can sense how much patience they have or assume how resentful they are at their jobs, and we can usually predict how the interaction is going to go. We are all instantly intuitive in this way. Why is that? It is because we often have these tendencies ourselves.

At first, it's hard to accept that the flaws I identify in others are often the same ones I have. My initial reaction is to be judgmental and to condemn other people's behavior, trying to separate myself from them in an attempt to feel superior. If I look just a little deeper, however, or give myself a few more minutes, I quickly find we're more similar than I realized. Being from Los Angeles, a ready example of this is in the driving habits of others. It's easy to get frustrated in congested traffic, and I'm quick to be annoyed at disrespectful drivers who cut in and out of traffic, or who won't let me into another lane. My annoyance quickly turns to chagrin, though, as I approach the next on-ramp and have to decide whether to let someone in or speed up and get in front of them. Funny how I can be just like the other drivers I was judging just moments ago.

I once heard that empathy is like sending out a sonar of feelings to another person and having it come back with pieces of yourself; this is the way we connect to and identify with others. It is through this same process that we are able to see our own character flaws reflected in the behaviors of others. Oftentimes, what we are most annoyed about in other people turns out to be the same qualities we have in ourselves. In this way, people become great teachers for us, often mirroring traits, tendencies, and flaws we also share. The next time you find yourself in judgment or annoyed with another person, ask yourself what you are spotting in them and if you can spot it in yourself as well. This is one of the best ways to develop self-awareness, as well as develop true empathy and understanding for others.

19

The way to make a mountain out of a molehill is to add dirt.

I t's amazing how we can sometimes turn small things into big things. A disagreement with a coworker can become a much bigger deal simply by stewing over it, working over what he or she might have meant, and then adding in previous perceived slights or incidents. Within hours, what could have been easily resolved suddenly becomes a full-on rift, which we continue to make worse by avoiding the person, or enlisting others to our side, or by talking behind the other person's back, and so on. Building up the mountain in this way happens with other molehills, too. A small noise the car starts making can lead us to worry about an expensive repair. A sensitive tooth can have us dreading a root canal. A spouse's careless offhand comment can lead us to wondering if this is the beginning of the end of the marriage. Overthinking a situation often leads to "adding dirt" in this way, and psychologists even have a word for it: catastrophizing.

Catastrophizing simply means to view or talk about an event or situation as worse than it actually is. It's something many of us may do to some extent, and there are several reasons for it. One can be when we're describing a situation to someone else, we want to make sure the other person feels the full strength of our frustration or fear over it. To get our point across, we exaggerate and make it worse than it really is. Doing so is a way to ensure the other person takes us seriously or gives us the comfort or reassurance we're looking for. Another reason we tend to catastrophize is as a coping skill to prepare ourselves for what we fear might be the worst outcome. How would we handle it? What would we do? By playing a scenario to its absolute worst end, we can mentally deal with it in advance. On a deeper level, it's also been theorized that our tendency to look for negative outcomes is a vestige of an earlier defense mechanism we developed when we were hunter-gatherers. In order to stay alive, it was in our benefit to search for danger and be on the alert for threats from the moment we opened our eyes. Perhaps this explains why some of us wake up and begin reviewing the possible pitfalls or challenges that await us in the day ahead. While this instinct to search for trouble or to imagine the worst might be a natural tendency, there are better ways of dealing with it.

One of the best strategies for avoiding catastrophizing might be summed up with the phrase, "Stop carrying it." This saying comes from a Zen story about two monks who come to a river crossing. As they prepare to cross, they notice the current is very strong, and then they see a young and beautiful woman struggling to cross. Because the monks have taken a vow not to speak to or touch women, they glance at each other, uncertain what to do. The young girl finally asks them if they could help her cross. The older monk immediately picks the girl up and carries her across. Hours later, the younger monk is clearly upset and finally faces the older monk and says, "I can't believe you carried that girl across the river! We're not supposed to touch women!" The older monk simply replies, "I set her down on the other side of the river; why are you still carrying her?"

To avoid making a mountain out of a molehill, it's best to stop carrying it, which is to say, to stop obsessing over it. Either take an action to address the situation or bring yourself back to the now by noticing what you are doing at the present moment and focusing your attention on that. It also helps to write down some options that you can revisit later when you're calmer. As mentioned, I always keep notebooks and scraps of paper around the house so I can get things out of my head and onto a to-do list for later. Doing these to clear your mind will prevent you from adding dirt onto something and making it a much bigger deal than it should be.

"I never imagined the greatest achievement in my life would be peace of mind."

—Unknown

We have been taught to strive for and to achieve things and that when we get them, we will feel a sense of accomplishment and peace. When we were little children, we certainly had a glimpse of how things could make us feel as we excitedly opened gifts on our birthdays and holidays. When we entered school, we set off on the path of trying to achieve good grades to build feelings of self-worth and accomplishment, or we sought validation by trying to make a sports team or get involved in a social club. As we began our career, the pursuit of happiness was tied to advancement in our jobs, or in making more money, or gaining more recognition. Once we started families, we often shifted our priorities to making sure our children got the gifts they wanted and achieved good grades or chose suitable careers or found the right spouse and started their own families. Throughout our lives, we labor under the belief that once we get something or accomplish something outside ourselves—whatever that looks like—then we will also achieve feelings of security, happiness, and the peace of mind that come with it.

Once all is said and done, however, some of us find that all these outside things have been nothing more than a persistent and elusive illusion.

As many people can attest—myself included—achieving all these things may bring temporary feelings of contentment, and even glimpses of happiness, yet these feelings often fade. Inevitably, new goals and certainly new challenges arise, which only extend the illusion of "Once I achieve this, then I'll finally be happy and feel at peace." The problem—and ironically, the solution—is that nothing outside of ourselves will ever permanently give us the sense of peace and contentment we all crave. Through the ages, spiritual teachers have taught us that those feelings of peace and happiness we seek are found inside of us, and our main goal in life is to find ways to discover and nurture the sense of peace we intrinsically have.

There are many ways to cultivate the inner peace that sits like a spark within us all. Developing or reviving a religious path or a spiritual practice is a wonderful starting point. Most of us have a sense of wonder or a longing to connect with something greater than ourselves, and there are many different paths of exploring what resonates with you. Nurturing these practices with meditation and prayer each morning or evening goes a long way to fanning those embers of peace and contentment, and even a regular practice of just five minutes spent in silence can make a significant difference throughout your day. Practicing gratitude or appreciating our lives, our spouses, our children, our friends—without judgment—also helps awaken the feelings of connection, belonging, and contentment we all long for. As we learn to go within ourselves to achieve the sense of meaning and purpose we once sought outside of ourselves, we discover an amazing gift: the greatest achievement of our lives might just be peace of mind, and we had access to it all along.

21

According to who?

A friend of mine was at a funeral the other day, and as she started taking a few pictures, someone came up to her and abruptly hissed, "You can't take photos at a funeral!" To which my friend immediately responded, "According to who?" She continued taking pictures, and those pictures have remained an important part of her memory of that day. As she and I were talking about this incident, she told me this is one of her favorite sayings, and she's found it to be a consistent way to challenge the status quo; she says it comes in handy in all types of situations.

We're all frequently admonished, advised, and bombarded with a lot of opinions as to what's right and what's wrong, and it's useful to consider, "According to who?" So much of what we hear is really just someone's opinion, and much of it has little bearing on us. Moreover, there are very few overarching rules to living that we must abide by and strictly follow. The next time you hear "You shouldn't," or "You can't," or "You're not supposed to," you should ask yourself, "According to who?"

Questioning authority or someone's opinion is what has led to some of the greatest discoveries and advances of humankind. Imagine if Columbus had listened when they told him he couldn't sail over the horizon, or if Galileo had listened to the prevailing wisdom that all planets and the sun revolved around the earth. Think about all the people who would have continued to die if Dr. Ignaz Semmel Weis had not fought against the obstinate prejudice against washing hands between surgeries and other medical procedures. Of course, you don't have to go back through history to reveal the tremendous usefulness of this quote.

Just look at your own life. How many times have you been told, warned, or even threatened with a piece of advice or strongly held opinion that you had the courage and the inner knowing to question? And how often have you looked beyond that advice and found that it wasn't true for you at all? I would venture to say you have plenty of proof of this, and that's why it's so helpful to incorporate this way of questioning as a useful tool for personal growth. Learning that what is right for one person may not be right for you is the beginning of self-awareness and, ultimately, individual happiness.

These days, whenever I have an idea, a dream, a goal, or just an intuitive feeling about trying something, I'm prepared for the naysayers to tell me, "You can't do that," or "You're not supposed to do that." I quickly reply, "According to who?" That usually stops them, and while it may not get them to change their opinion on the spot, it does something more important for me: it allows me to move beyond preconceived boundaries and to reach for alternative ways to live a more fulfilled and expansive life—a life that is free to explore, discover, and find what works best for me.

Look out the
other person's window.

In his wonderful book written for new therapists, *The Gift of Therapy*, Irvin D. Yalom, MD, relates a story one of his patients told him that helped increase his understanding of "accurate empathy" (a term defined by the therapist, Carl Rogers, as meaning "the listener's effort to hear the other person deeply, accurately, and nonjudgmentally"). The patient was a young woman being driven to college by her naysaying father. She was looking forward to this time alone with him, but as they drove down the highway, the father looked out his window and complained about all the trash and debris in the creek alongside the highway. She, on the other hand, looking out her own window, saw the beautiful countryside and a creek that was clear and that meandered gently through the forest opening. Frustrated, she shut down, and they continued the multihour drive in silence.

A while later, she made the same trip alone, and she was astounded to see there were two creeks—one on each side of the road. Glancing out both windows this time, she saw the other creek was indeed polluted and littered with garbage, just as her father had described it. By the time she had the experience of seeing out her father's window, and thus understanding his point of view, he had already passed. Dr. Yalom says this story made a big impact on him, and he reminds new therapists to always see the patient's side of things, to look through their windows, as it were.

This story has always stuck with me. Whenever I'm with people who have different points of view or who have very different reactions to similar events than I do, I think back to this woman's experience. I quietly wonder what the view looks like outside the other person's window. Practicing empathy this way allows me to be more curious than offended or judgmental, and when I'm able to remain open to the other person's experience, I'm always fascinated by what I learn. Inevitably, there is a lot more behind someone's reaction to things, including their conditioning, upbringing, fears, hopes—the whole range of emotions that drive my reactions as well.

The world is filled with different people, from different cultures and backgrounds, and we are all looking at the world through our own windows. By taking the time to look out another's, you might just be surprised by their view.

23

When I feed the problem, it grows; when I feed the solution, it grows.

Each morning when we wake up, we have a choice as to what we focus on and where we place our attention. Life always has its challenges and problems, but it also has its solutions and opportunities as well. One useful tool I've found that helps direct my focus is deciding what kind of questions I'm going to ask myself. I've found that "why" questions tend to keep me in the problem. For example: Why did this or that have to happen? Why can't I ever catch a break? When we keep asking "why" questions about other parts of our lives, the problems in those areas can grow, too.

When we ask different questions that begin with "what," "when," "where," and "who," solutions begin to appear, such as:

- *What* are three things I can do to resolve this?
- *Where* can I find some answers or relief to this problem?
- *When* would be the best time to try those solutions?
- *Who* can I ask that might be able to help me with this today, or who has experience I can borrow or leverage?

Asking these types of helpful questions not only leads to solutions I may not have thought about, but by focusing on them rather than the problem, my perception of the problem changes, and my attitude becomes more positive. By reminding ourselves that we may not have control over the problem or situation, but we do have a choice as to where we focus our thinking, life becomes a lot more empowering.

In addition to feeding the solution by reframing the question, I sometimes like to imagine I can help others do this as well. A fun habit I developed years ago, and something you can try yourself, is to randomly smile at people I see when I'm out in public: at markets, airports, parking lots—anywhere, really. People are often preoccupied, deep in their thoughts, and they can look serious and sometimes even angry. Scurrying around, sporting a scowl, I wonder if they are deeply involved in asking themselves the "why" questions and so dwelling on the problems in their lives. As I pass them, I attempt to make eye contact, and when they look at me, I give them a big, warm smile and watch as their face brightens and they smile back. I hope that by helping people change their focus, even for that instant, it helps them shift their thinking to something more positive. It's a wonderful habit to get into, and it makes both you and the other person feel better.

Life will always have its ups and downs, and we'll always be able to handle the down times better by choosing the kinds of questions we ask. When you wake up tomorrow, ask yourself what you are going to focus on: the problems or the solutions? Either one will grow in accordance with how you feed it.

24

"Each day comes bearing its own gifts. Untie the ribbons."

—Ruth Ann Schabacker

My older brother has an interesting way of describing vacations. He calls the experience "clicking the kaleidoscope." He says that as soon as you go to a new place, everything seems as if it has shifted, and you're instantly able to see even routine things as if they were new, colorful, and exciting. The wonder of life returns.

When my wife and I lived on the West Coast, Hawaii was a frequent vacation spot for us. I loved going to the Starbucks each morning for a venti Pike Place and then heading to the beach to sit on the sand and listen to the waves lapping the shore. I gazed with amazement as the sun slowly rose over Diamond Head, its rays blazing in all directions, and watched the early morning surfers paddle to greet the rolling waves in the bay. I'd sip my coffee and breathe in the salty sea air. I could feel the gifts the day offered me. I look forward to vacations to help me regain this fresh perspective on the world and to be reminded of the gifts that are literally around me all the time. Unfortunately, the vacation experience fades once I return home, and a different reality takes its place.

Almost as soon as I put the suitcases down, the responsibilities and routines of life take over and off I go. There's laundry to do, things around the house to attend to, and then the impending reality of Monday morning and work. Wrapped up in the business of our lives, it's too easy to forget the gifts and instead get buried in the familiar minutiae. We tend to put our heads down and go through the motions: another quick breakfast, the same commute to work, eight hours at the desk, and then home to the chores and little challenges of family relationships. On the weekends, we use what little time we have to run errands, take care of bigger chores, and try to enjoy what downtime we have left. Monday looms in the background, and soon we start the new week the way we ended the last, immersed in our routines. Life through the lens of routine seems monotone, and the click of the kaleidoscope is but a distant memory. Luckily, there are easy ways to re-click it, without having to wait for the next vacation.

A helpful habit to develop is to search for and discover the many gifts, the joys, the beauty, and the surprises that each day offers. While it is easy to get into a rut, it's also easy to get out of it and to renew our perspective in simple ways: We can take a different route to work, observing the new scenery and maybe even trying a new coffee shop along the way. At work, we can choose to eat outside and see how many birds we can spot; we can go to lunch with a different coworker or try a new restaurant, or even order something different at the regular lunch spot. Mixing up our evening routines is rewarding as well: we can take the family out to an early dinner and movie, try bowling one Thursday night, or take our spouse on an unexpected date night.

Each variation in your routine is like clicking the kaleidoscope of your life. These clicks help you recognize the gifts you have and remind you that you don't have to wait for your next vacation to untie the ribbons and rediscover the wonder each day holds.

25

"Aging is an extraordinary process whereby you become the person you always should have been."

—David Bowie

For much of our lives, other people have a huge influence on how we come to know ourselves and build our sense of who we are. During our childhood, our parents guide, shape, and influence us as they teach us to speak and then answer our unending questions. Throughout elementary school they remain almost inseparable from us, and during these years we feel lost and even afraid when they're not around. Through middle school and high school, we begin distancing ourselves from our parents and are more influenced by our friends and teachers. Suddenly, a whole new world opens before us, and our emerging sense of self begins to explore and grow. It's an exciting time as well as a challenging and confusing one.

For many of us, our college years are when we finally feel that we have come into our own. Our confidence swells, and we begin to get a real idea of who we might be and what we want to do with the rest of our lives. While still influenced by parents, teachers, friends, and our own growing sense of self, we make choices we feel are right for us, and we begin our professional and adult lives. Then something unexpected happens for many of us. Once we embark on what we think will be our forever career, the one we studied and prepared for, we sometimes find that it isn't what we thought it was, or what we wanted, and that it isn't who we *really* are. So begins another great search for self, for meaning, for fulfillment—the journey of our lives.

This is where the wisdom of aging comes in. When I think of David Bowie's career as a musician, one thing that defined him over the years was change. Bowie's albums are all different: different musical styles, different personas, explorations into different aspects of his changing self. One thing that remained constant for Bowie, however, was his love of books and of reading. During his career, he didn't get a chance to read as much as he'd like to. When he grew older, he spent increasing amounts of time with his family, and he indulged his love of reading. He has been known to say that there was nothing he'd rather spend his time doing than reading a good book. Quite a quiet life for one of rock's biggest stars.

While I've not been a rock star, I've certainly changed throughout my life as well: the different jobs and careers I've had have all given me greater clarity as to who I really am, what makes me genuinely happy—and it's not all the things I had been taught to chase or acquire. As I get older, I listen more closely to my authentic self, follow its direction, and allow myself to go down the path it whispers to me. The more I do, the more peaceful I become, and the more satisfied and happier I am. I've become more the person I was always meant to be, and that's been the wonderful thing about aging.

I only wish I had followed that road less traveled earlier in my life. I suppose it's a regret many people have, and there is fear attached to doing that: Would we be okay? Would we be happy? Could we afford that different life direction? I once read a quote by John Grisham that addressed many of those questions for me. He said, "Live your life the way you want. You'll figure it out." That has certainly been my experience. Just know that it's never too early—or too late—to pursue your own path, the road that truly speaks to you. After all, you're going to end up there anyway as you age. Why not start now?

26

I don't have a rewind button in my life, but I do have a pause.

E mail, texting, social media posts: there are a lot of ways for us to make our feelings known quickly. Unfortunately, when we're upset or when something happens that triggers the urge to let those feelings out, especially when we're feeling slighted, it's too easy for us to text or email our hurt or angry feelings or to retaliate inappropriately. Once we press "send" or "post," it's done. We can't get it back or rewind what we've just said. Many of us have been on the receiving end of these kinds of communications, and we know the stress and damage they can do to our relationships.

It's not just the receiver who feels the sting of the response, either. Whenever I've acted impetuously and fired off an angry or spiteful text or email, I feel the effects as well. After calming down, I'm enveloped in an emotional hangover of guilt and shame. At times like these, I've sorely wished for a rewind button, but as we all know, we can't get it back.

That's when the pause button comes in handy. A friend once explained this concept to me, and it has saved me time and time again. He explained that it works like this: to start with, you have to remember that there are going to be times when your emotions will flare—relationships are just that way. Someone will disappoint you, or purposely go against you, or frustrate you in some way, and your reaction will be to strike back. He told me that when this happens, it's okay to write that email—just don't send it. If you have to respond—have to "get it out"—go ahead and do so. Again, just don't send it. Instead, save it as a draft; it even helps to not put the person's email address in yet (this saves you from accidentally sending it). After you've written and saved the draft, pause and walk away, and wait at least twenty-four hours before you read what you've written.

What you might find once you've calmed down is that you feel a lot differently as your emotions have settled. I personally give myself a week before I read what I've written, and a lot happens during that week to help me gain some perspective. Sometimes, the other person will apologize or will reach out to clarify things, and often I'll receive more information that will help me understand what the other person really meant. What always happens, though, is that I'm grateful I didn't press send. Pausing in this way has saved me from damaging friendships and has saved me from escalating a misunderstanding. It's also saved me from the emotional fallout that can affect me for months, if not years.

As you move through the relationships in your life, remember that while you don't have a rewind button, you do have a pause. You can use the pause when you're tempted to fire off an email or text, and you can also use the pause if you're face-to-face with someone and feel the temperature rising. By giving yourself time like this to recover your center and your perspective, you'll be in a much better place in a few days after you've been able to process your feelings and come up with an appropriate way of responding. Doing so will help both you and the other person immeasurably, and it will make your life more peaceful and your relationships more loving. It will also keep you from wishing you had a rewind button.

27

"Be kind, for everyone you meet is fighting a great battle."

—Ian Maclaren

I have a longtime acquaintance who hangs out with the same group of friends as I do. He is well dressed and professional and is a really nice guy, with a genuine smile on his face and a kind word for all he meets. One day, he showed up looking a little out of sorts, tired, and slightly disheveled, and we asked him what was going on. He told us he has a special-needs son who has been disabled since birth. His son is eleven now, and he's been suffering all his young life with brain swelling, and the night before, they rushed him to the hospital where he is staying while they determine whether or not to operate again. The man related this story very matter-of-factly, yet underneath it, I could hear the years of struggle he'd been through, the fear and desperation he had fought hard to control and conceal. We were all very supportive, of course, and I was amazed that I had no idea he was dealing with all this.

When I read today's quote, I instantly connected with its great truth. My experience is that as soon as I sit down with someone and get to know them, really listen to them, I'm surprised by how much they are dealing with. Challenges such as managing the care of elderly parents is something we may all face at some point in our lives.

When we marry, we often have a whole other family to care about as well. Some people who have children deal not only with the normal challenges of parenting but also with special situations and needs that alter their lives, requiring sacrifices that can seem unimaginable to many of us. People and families sometimes deal with addiction of a loved one and serious illnesses of spouses, family members, children, and even themselves. We have all heard stories of people dying suddenly, and many of them much too young, leaving a loving family and small children. No one is immune to these real-life scenarios, and many of us have been touched by these kinds of tragedies.

When we meet people in public, at work, at parties or other gatherings, what we sometimes forget is that many are fighting a great battle of their own. It's so easy to criticize someone who is acting rudely or misbehaving in other ways. What we often fail to consider is what that person might be going through. Once, I drove behind an elderly couple who were going way too slow for the hurry that I was in that day. Just as I was about to jump on my horn, the friend I was with stopped me and said, "Let them be. For all you know, the wife is driving her husband to the memory-care facility to admit him. This may be the last drive they'll ever be able to take together. They don't need an obnoxious jerk behind them at a moment like this." When I thought about it in this light, I gained a deep sense of compassion and respect for the couple in front of me. I connected with the shared journey we all go through, and I remembered that my job is to be kind to the people I meet.

Kindness is the one gift we can all give one another, and it's the one gift we are all deserving of, always. While you may not know much about the people you meet or interact with briefly in public, you can be sure of one thing: they all have situations and people in their lives that sometimes take unimaginable levels of courage to deal with. If someone seems ill-mannered or angry, rather than react to that, offer them a kind word or a warm gesture instead. Your kindness will surely lighten their burden, even for just a moment.

28

"Don't let what you can't do stop you from what you can do."

—John Wooden

This wonderful reminder from UCLA's famous basketball coach John Wooden has helped me accomplish so much, especially when I thought I couldn't accomplish anything at all. In the face of adversity or setbacks, it reminds me to focus on what is still possible. Recently, I joined the gym to get in better shape, and after a couple of weeks, I tweaked my shoulder. My first response was to stop going until it felt better, and then I remembered John Wooden's words. I asked myself what I could still do at the gym that didn't involve my shoulder. Turns out, a lot! Cardio, legs, abs, and much more. By reframing my shoulder injury from what I couldn't do to what I still *could* do, I was able to stay on track while my shoulder healed. Likewise, when my schedule changes and I have to travel for business, I simply pack my gym clothes and make sure I schedule time in the hotel gym before or after my workday.

Many of us find ourselves in similar situations. Perhaps we can't afford the time or money to pursue a graduate degree full-time, so we dismiss the idea of doing what we can do: part-time, night classes, online courses, or even summer sessions. Doing it this way, we can still accomplish our goal and feel empowered while doing it.

This same concept can be applied to many areas of our lives, and it's important to remember because challenges will always come up for us. There will always be things that get in the way of our plans, and we will all suffer disappointment. The key is to constantly stay focused on what we can do rather than on the problem of what we can't do now. This is how we keep moving forward toward our goals and how we achieve and maintain the positive attitude we need to keep trying.

In addition to applying this concept to our personal lives, it's also how we can make a significant contribution in the lives of others. When we think about all the problems in the world, it can be overwhelming. How can we help any situation or help anyone at all when so many people need so much? I used to think this way as well until I heard a story about two friends who were walking along the beach. The tide was out, and on the beach were hundreds of stranded starfish. One of the guys bent down, picked one up and threw it into the sea. The other guy said, "What did you do that for? There are hundreds of these things, and that's not going to make a difference." The other guy replied, "It made a difference for that one."

What I love about this story is that it reminds me that while I may not be able to cure world hunger or solve the climate crisis, I can still do my part to make a difference on some level. If we all did what we could do, instead of being discouraged by what we can't, the world would be a much better place.

29

We don't need more to be thankful for, we need to be more thankful.

M any of us fall into the illusion that if we just had more of something, or a better something, or if we never had to worry about money, then we'd be happy and secure. The sad truth is that often when we get the object of our desire, it rarely satisfies us, and soon we're off looking for the next something. One sure way to center yourself and become more thankful for all the things you already have is to write a gratitude list. You may have heard of it: it's where you make a list of all the things that make your life comfortable or more enjoyable that you tend to overlook or not appreciate enough. These can be necessities like having a roof over your head or access to fresh water, or things that would make life easier, like a car or computer, etc. We are surrounded with material items that we take for granted every day, yet we seldom stop to think about the hundreds of millions of other people in the world who either don't have access to these "luxury" items or can't afford them.

Material items are just the start, though. Most of us are rich in many other ways as well, including having loving family and friends or a job or career in which we get to contribute and derive a sense of identity and satisfaction. There is our health—most of us have enough health to walk without pain, to see and hear and touch and smell—small miracles that other people have been deprived of. The point of making a gratitude list is to reset our perception, to restore our sense of thankfulness for being alive and for the many blessings we already have.

Making a list of things we're thankful for also helps to relieve anxiety when we're in fear of either losing something we have or of not having enough of something we think we need. If we find ourselves sliding into financial insecurity, we can instantly make a gratitude list around finances. You can start by acknowledging that all your bills are currently paid, and you probably have enough money in your pocket (or room on a credit card) to feed yourself and your family today and in the foreseeable future. Next, if you're employed, you can list that, as well as the paycheck you're sure to receive soon. If you're unemployed, just remind yourself of all the other times you were without work and how you eventually found that next job. Most financial fear comes from projecting ourselves far into the future, yet once we list the many financial advantages we have today (the ability to earn income, any savings we have, and even access to loans when needed, etc.), we see that everything is okay.

Whenever I do this kind of financial gratitude list, I'm able to acknowledge that up until this point in my life, and despite feeling scared about finances in the past, I've always been taken care of and things have turned out all right. As I review my gratitude list, I feel the fear and insecurity recede, and after ten to twenty items, I feel more at peace and my anxiety is replaced by a deep sense of thankfulness for what I *do* have.

Making specific gratitude lists for the areas we're in fear about works with nearly everything. Whenever you have physical fear, just write a list of twenty-five things around your health that you already have and are grateful for. Chances are, you have the gift of health in many areas, and you probably have access to doctors and medicines and therapies that can offer you relief and even eventual cures. If you think that twenty-five items are too many, just start the list anyway and watch how quickly things add up and how easy it becomes. Writing gratitude lists is a great way to start your day and a wonderful way to remind yourself that you don't need more things to be thankful for, you simply have to take the time to count all the things you *already are* thankful for.

You've given me a lot to think about. Let me get back to you on that.

How many times has someone asked you to do something you didn't want to do or pressured you to give an answer or opinion you weren't ready to give? Or worse, how often have you given in to their pressure, answered the best you could—or in the way you thought they wanted to hear—without thinking it through? Then later, while you're quiet and have the time to give it careful consideration, you realize you would have given a completely different answer? Then off you go, role-playing in your head and coming up with several different responses or ways of responding that reflect how you truly feel and coming up with answers or responses that you wish you would have said if only you had had the time to process it.

This happens to all of us, and it's especially common with family members with whom we often have little defense and few healthy boundaries. I once heard that your family knows how to push your buttons because they are the ones who installed them. Many times, when confronted by family or intimate others, we quickly assess what they are getting at and then give them the answers we think they want to hear.

Someone taught me a wonderful answer to use whenever I'm feeling pressured to respond when I'm not ready. She said whenever you're feeling that way, simply give yourself time by saying, "You know, you've given me a lot to think about. Let me get back to you on that." Responding in this way gives me the precious time I need to sit with my feelings, discuss them with others, and then arrive at an answer that is in alignment with my truth. It also helps me avoid the inevitable consequences of agreeing to something or saying something that I regret later.

Variations of this can also be used if someone asks me for a *yes* or *no* answer to which I'm not ready to commit. Moss Hart once said: "All the mistakes I ever made were when I wanted to say 'No' and said 'Yes.'" Learning to say, "Let me check on something and get back to you," or "Not sure, let me get back to you," has saved me from saying yes—and wishing later that I hadn't done so. Try these yourself the next time you're feeling pressured or confronted by someone to answer when you're not ready to. It will save you a lot of second-guessing and regret later on.

"We will be known forever by the tracks we leave."

—Native American proverb

We spend a lot of our lives trying to accumulate and accomplish things to build our sense of self, to feel secure,
and to be happy. For years, my young ego believed in
the saying "He who dies with the most toys wins," and I set my sights
on getting the next better thing, like a bigger apartment or nicer
house; a sleeker, more expensive car; or the latest tech device—there
was no end to what I needed to feel better. Many of us continue to
chase these kinds of things, sure that they'll complete us, give our
lives meaning in some way, yet as many of us have found, the more
we acquire or accomplish, the emptier we sometimes feel.

Being in a relationship fills us in a different way. Having children
or being an uncle or aunt gives us an opportunity to extend ourselves,
and this leads to a deeper happiness and to a sense of belonging. By
stepping outside of ourselves, involving ourselves in the lives of others, we are completed by the love and caring we give to another. In
many ways, this is the first feeling of real meaning we experience,
and it's the first hint that giving, rather than getting, is the path to the
meaning we've sought in our lives.

As I've grown older, the saying "You can only keep what you give away" has taken on a new meaning. Rather than by accumulating, I've found that it is in the giving away—my time, my experience, by helping others—that I've felt the feelings of peace and meaning that I once looked for elsewhere. What we leave behind is truly the only thing that we can keep, because it's the only thing others will remember us by. No one will care how big our house was, though they will remember the time we had coffee with them and listened when they were going through a hard time.

These days, I'm much less concerned with what I can get than what I can contribute. William James once said, "The use of a life is to spend it for something that outlasts it." What outlasts our lives? It's what we leave behind. Think about it: do you remember who taught you to ride a bike, drive a car, or who was with you when you were the most down in your life? These are the moments that mean more than all the material accomplishments that we spend so much time trying to get. I think that when a grandparent sees the spark of light shine in the innocent eyes of their grandchildren, they have seen into the true meaning of their lives.

"You can't take it with you" is another saying that reminds us that what's important in life are the tracks we leave. If you want to cultivate a sense of real meaning in your life, look outward, toward those in your life to whom you can give love, time, and help. Those memories will be the ones that you are remembered by.

32

Humility is not thinking less about yourself; rather, it's thinking about yourself less.

H umility is a misunderstood concept. Many feel that if they were humble, they wouldn't get what they wanted, that others would take advantage of them or get ahead of them professionally, and so on. Social media doesn't help with this perception either: Instagram, Facebook, TikTok, and YouTube influencers all vie for attention, and it seems like you have to promote yourself more and more if you want to get noticed. Practicing humility appears to be the antithesis of what it takes to get ahead, to be popular, and to be successful.

Think about it for a moment, though: Who are you most drawn to? Those who constantly talk about themselves and who can't wait to share what they're doing, where they're going, or what they have? Or are you more attracted to those close friends and family members who are more focused on you, who are more interested in what you're going through and what you're thinking and feeling? I have several people in my life (and I hope you do, too) whom I consider to be truly humble, who know themselves and are comfortable with who they are. They have no need to brag or make themselves more than they are; instead, they have a deep sense of humility, which allows them to be open to me and my experiences. It reminds me of a saying: "When you are less full of yourself, you have more room for others." I'm attracted to these people because I know they care about me and have room in their hearts for me. This is what true humility means.

There are great benefits to practicing humility. The first is that as soon as you take the focus off yourself, you become happier and more at peace. Released from the burden of self, you are liberated from the constant need to prove yourself, impress others, and get noticed. Once you accept yourself for who you are, a calm descends, and you become more open to others. That is one of the greatest gifts of all: your ability to help and to have empathy for another human being.

The way to practice humility is easy enough. When you find that you're obsessed with yourself or scheming to get ahead or worried over what you don't have, simply ask yourself what you can give or do for another person instead. The moment you take the focus off yourself, you'll find that you are practicing humility. In that moment, you'll receive the key to long-lasting contentment—and so will those around you.

33

"The oldest voice in the world is the wind."

—Donald C. Peattie

I heard this quote years ago, and it resonated with me deeply. I looked up at the trees in the forest and watched the leaves flutter and the branches sway. I smiled as I listened to the wind and watched it move invisibly through the woods. Instantly, I was present, grounded, and happy to be alive. As I watched this ancient movement, I felt both a part of our planet's history and acutely aware of being in the here and now. I slowed down from my hectic life and took in the wonder of the world around me.

My awareness soon extended to the various bushes, plants, and flowers in the garden, all reaching toward the sun overhead. I noticed a bench I had passed by many times, and I decided to sit for a moment and to simply be. People sped by, many with their heads down, staring into their phones, the same way I had countless times before. Soon, I became aware of the birds—the original tweeters—singing to one another, flittering from branch to branch. That's when it hit me: the peace I'd sought for so long, the calm, the ability to be present and enjoy life was all around me, waiting for me to stop and take it in.

Somehow, life has become more and more complicated, more and more demanding, despite the promise of technology to free us and make our lives simpler. Before email, we'd write and mail letters, and once we put our pens down, we'd patiently wait for the response and bring our attention back to what we were doing in the now. Our communication was softer; it gave us time to reflect and respond with the benefit of time and attention. Today, however, we are bombarded with emails and texts, combined with the compulsion to keep checking for a response, which keeps us chained to our devices. Instead of freeing us, technology finds ways of ensnaring us, occupying us, and stealing our thoughts and diminishing our awareness.

Blaise Pascal, the French philosopher, once said that "all of humanity's problems stem from man's inability to sit quietly in a room alone." If we want to cultivate the ability to be present, to be at peace with ourselves, then it's important for us to find ways to disconnect from the demands and stresses of our lives, to rediscover the calm and simple beauty that surround us. The next time you are walking and see a bench, or find that you have time to slow down a moment, turn your phone off, take a seat, and listen for the oldest voice in the world. You just might find that the peace you seek has always been available to you, whispering through the trees.

34

"We don't see things as they are, we see them as we are."

—Anais Nin

I t's interesting how we can see the familiar things in our lives—our parents or spouses, our jobs, our homes or neighborhoods—and watch them change from day-to-day. Sometimes we feel grateful for our work, feel accomplished and appreciated, yet on other days, we find ourselves wishing we were doing something else or even resentful over the lack of support we feel. The same can be true of our relationships and even how we feel about our material possessions—some days we're happy with them while other days we think we need newer or better ones. When this happens, it's useful to ask ourselves what has changed within us.

A common expression is "Did you get up on the wrong side of the bed this morning?" You know how it goes. One day you wake up feeling rested, hopeful, even empowered; other days you might feel a little less energetic, or perhaps your regular routine feels like a rut, and your responsibilities feel heavier. Nothing outside of yourself has changed significantly, though your attitude has. At these times, it's helpful to examine how you are looking at things in your life, and as you do, you'll discover that by changing your perspective, the world changes as well.

Whenever I'm feeling out of sorts—when the neighbor's activity seems too loud or disruptive, or my clients seem too demanding, or the weather is too hot or too cold—I play a game with myself. I ask myself how I would feel about these things if I adopted the opposite attitude than what I have right now. I remember the pleasant feelings I have when I go out and visit with my neighbor, or I remind myself how grateful I am to have clients and how my role is to be of service to them. If it's raining, I grab an umbrella and stand in my driveway and soak in the smell of the rain and watch as the plants and grass drink in the nourishment they need.

As I go through this exercise, I feel the magic in today's saying: as I shift my perspective, and therefore my outlook, I see this change reflected in the circumstances around me. In this instant, I'm reminded that the only things I can truly control are my attitude and my actions. When I work to change these, the whole world changes along with them. Whenever you find yourself disturbed or annoyed or not as peaceful as you'd like to be, simply search out your current attitude and ask yourself how different things would be if you adopted a new one. Remembering that we can change the things around us by changing ourselves first restores not only a sense of control over our lives, it actually changes our lives as well.

There are no victims, only volunteers. You always have a choice.

We all have obligations we feel bound to fulfill, and at first, it doesn't seem as if we have much choice. Family obligations, especially, run deep. Years ago, I was faced with a situation with my stepfather in which I felt trapped; I definitely didn't think I had a choice. He had a stroke one day and was put in a nursing home. It suddenly fell on me and my sister to bring him home each weekend, and soon the strain of that became too much. He was in a wheelchair and incontinent, and I dreaded weekends. I was scared that something would go wrong and was overcome by the physical and mental toll it was taking. Yet, I didn't feel I had a choice—until I spoke with my therapist about it.

I'll never forget the shock I had when, after telling her I had to continue picking my stepfather up and taking him back, that it was my duty to my mother, etc., she looked at me and said, "No, you don't *have* to do it. You are *choosing* to do it." I stared at her incredulously and began to argue, but she cut me off. She explained by asking me some questions.

"Do you have the proper training to care for an invalid?"

"No," I answered.

"Do you have the appropriate vehicle to carry a wheelchair-bound person?" No, again, I answered.

After this discussion, she tasked me with finding the proper help, and once I did, my brothers and sister pooled our resources and found an affordable—and capable—person to transport and properly care for him.

This was a big shift for me. My therapist continued to work with me in examining the other areas of my life where I felt like a victim. What I came to realize is that I make choices in every area of my life—where I live, whom I choose to be in relationships with, etc.— we all do. While it seems convenient sometimes to blame our circumstances or obligations, the truth is we're all volunteers. We always have a choice.

Sometimes there are situations that we may not be able to change right away—someone in prison is a good example, as are jobs or relationships we may choose not to leave at the moment—yet even in these situations, we have a choice over our attitudes and actions. Do we take care of ourselves physically and emotionally? Do we treat ourselves kindly, or do we beat ourselves up and abuse ourselves and those around us? Have we found acceptance of the situation or the other person for who they are? Have we learned to detach ourselves from them with love in our hearts? Once we look at the choices we do have, and once we make more loving choices over how we handle them and ourselves, we free ourselves from victimhood and find empowerment over our own lives.

If you find yourself in situations that make your life unmanageable, ask yourself what your choices are. Just acknowledging that there are different options will relieve the feeling you may have of being trapped or of being a victim. While it's a hard truth to accept at first, we are all volunteers in our lives. Recognizing this is the first step to personal freedom and the path to eventual peace.

How to guarantee you'll
be unhappy.

Many of us seek more happiness in our lives and more feelings of calm, peace, and connectedness. We work hard to
afford the things we think will make us more comfortable. We try to build active social lives with friends and family, try
to give back whenever we can, and when we do, we feel better about
our lives. But if you ever find yourself feeling down, disconnected, or
plain unhappy, you might want to examine this guaranteed formula
for unhappiness.

This method for cultivating unhappiness comes from one of
my favorite spiritual authors, Emmet Fox, and if you haven't read
his work yet, I highly recommend you do. This technique is simple,
works every time, and in the past, I've fallen into it without even noticing. And it's simple: think only about yourself. It helps to isolate so
you can give yourself full attention, but if you have a busy life, then
you can focus on yourself during any downtime: brushing your teeth,
commuting to work, and my personal favorite, lying in bed at night
and rolling over regrets of the past or fear of the future are good places
to start. There are many areas that are ripe to produce the desired
result, and I find that the past is usually a good place to start.

Think about your upbringing, and how much better your life
would have been if only your parents had supported or understood

you more. Think about your siblings and how unfairly they treated you. Jump around a little, focus on all the relationships in which you acted selfishly, all the poor choices you made, and the countless opportunities that you missed. My favorite is to preface these memories with "If only I hadn't," or "Why did he/she treat me that way?" This is always a good way to access self-pity, and this goes a long way to keeping you unhappy. If you continue to think deeply enough, you'll find there is a gold mine of slights and hurts and misunderstandings when you were growing up. Remember and relive the emotional impact of all your hurt feelings and stew in your old resentments. The past can keep you busy for a long time, and each time you visit it, you'll likely find something more to dwell on and regret.

Another good place to go is into the future. Sometimes, I'll find myself deep in fear as I think about how little time I have left, about how little money and security I really have. As I go down this road, it's easy to think about how I'll probably never be able to make up for the time I squandered. As I continue to dwell on myself and my certain ruin, I can picture myself homeless and alone.

Your health is a great place to dwell on as well. Think about how the years have affected you, of all the things you can no longer do, about all the aches and pains you have, or about all the illnesses you might get—or might already have but don't know about yet.

As you can see, it's easy to be unhappy. Using the above method for even a short while will work, and in no time, you'll notice a change in your attitude. If you don't have success the first time you do this, then repeat it often throughout the day or week, and I guarantee you'll succeed in feeling restless, irritable, and thoroughly unhappy. Fortunately, something else is also true: you can immediately restore a sense of happiness, peace, and fulfillment by doing the opposite.

The fastest way to feel better is to take the focus off yourself and seek to connect with and help others. Reach out to someone and ask them how a problem or situation they were dealing with the last time you met is working out. Then, listen to them—really listen; ask more questions if necessary, and get them to open up and take in what they are sharing with you. If you're at work or at home with others, ask yourself how you can be of service to those around you. Do something, anything, to help someone else. The magic in this strategy is that when you are out of yourself and into others you will feel the sense of connection and contribution that will bring you contentment. Most of all, you'll stop thinking about yourself. And that is the number-one ingredient to avoiding unhappiness.

37

"To attain knowledge, add things every day. To attain wisdom, remove things every day."

—Lao Tzu

In school, we cram in as many facts, dates, and events as we can to gather knowledge and pass the upcoming quiz or test. We memorize complex mathematical formulas, and we read through the curriculum of great works in literature in the hope of being better informed. Once our formal education is over, we begin a new phase of learning and try to acquire as much information about our jobs and careers as we can. This pursuit of knowledge has been drilled into many of us from the beginning of our lives, and we often feel that if we just knew more, then we'd be more successful, happier, or more competent.

In my forties, I went on a binge to acquire more knowledge in the field of psychology. I went back to school to get a graduate degree as a marriage and family therapist and felt sure I would be more successful if I learned more theory. The more I learned, however, the more I realized how much I didn't know. Each new school of thought—behaviorism, psychoanalysis, humanism, narrative therapy, and others—was like a new wormhole that led me into deeper levels of a field of study. I was acquiring knowledge quickly; however, when I sat and listened to clients, I found that my knowledge was limited and didn't translate into the wisdom I needed to be as effective as I would have liked.

At this point in my life, I realized that the path to wisdom wasn't found in books or memorizing or learning new facts and theories. It didn't come from adding anything at all. Instead, it came from letting go of what I thought I knew. It came from learning to listen to the experience, feelings, and unique viewpoints of others. If I truly wanted to help people, I needed to empty myself of much of the knowledge that I had spent so much time and energy trying to acquire. I needed to learn how to be more open instead.

Around this time, I heard a Zen story that perfectly captured this concept. A young student of Zen came to a village to meet with a renowned Zen master and to share a cup of tea. When they sat down, the young man bubbled with enthusiasm and was anxious to impress the Zen master with what he had studied and knew about the practice of Zen. As the student began talking, the master poured tea into his cup—and he kept pouring until the cup overflowed and tea began spreading over the table and dripped down to the floor. The student, aghast at what was happening, stopped speaking and told the master that he was spilling tea. At that point, the master stopped pouring and told the student that he was like the full cup of tea. The master told him that he held so much knowledge that there was no point in trying to pour any wisdom into him.

That's when I got it: when I am too full of myself and the knowledge I have, I stop being open to the ideas, thoughts, beliefs, and perspectives of others. If I wish to attain more wisdom, I need to empty my cup each day and allow others to pour their world into me. By releasing the knowledge we've accumulated, we can begin to take in the wisdom that surrounds us. This is when our true education begins.

38

Bring the body,
the mind will follow.

This is a simple yet valuable strategy for improving your attitude and feeling better in general. Sometimes our minds can be our own worst enemy, advising us not to do the things that make us feel better, like being more social or getting more active. Instead, it tells us to just stay home, to mute our phones, to isolate, and to spend hours on the couch alone binge-watching the newest trending series. When we follow its advice at these times, we get the inevitable result: we feel more sluggish or slightly down, and we tend to withdraw even more. If we bring the body, however, the mind will often snap out of its tendency to be alone, and soon we'll be glad we did.

An excellent example of this is going to the gym. There are plenty of times when I don't feel like getting dressed for, driving to, and working out at the gym. My mind tells me that I've got a hundred better options at home, and besides, I went yesterday (or three times last week). If I listen to my mind at these times, then it's easy to just stay home. Heck, I might not go for days or even months if I waited to feel like going! However, the moment I head to the gym, move my body, and get the endorphins going, I'm always pumped up and glad I went. I leave the gym invigorated and happy to be alive. Just moving the body in this way ignites the mind.

A friend and I were talking about this phenomenon, and she told me she has an expression for it. She calls it, "Taking contrary action." She says she has found that doing the opposite of what her mind tells her to do often works out for the best and ends up making her feel better. She says if she's invited out with friends and doesn't want to go, she says yes anyway. Invariably, she has a great time, and just like with the gym, she's happy she went out.

For years now, I've been practicing contrary action. It's been helpful for little decisions, like whether I should spend an hour cleaning a part of the house or call or text a few friends, and for bigger things like moving to another part of the country or finally starting a business. I've shared this technique with many friends and clients, and they always report feeling better when they take the opposite action.

Ultimately, our minds sometimes do "have a mind of their own." The quickest way to change them is to bring the body and take an action anyway. My experience is that the mind will change by engaging in the activity, and it'll be happy I brought it along.

39

Just what am I afraid of?

There are times when the little things in our lives can cause us a lot of stress or when inconsequential things can cause oversized reactions. We can be standing in a line that is moving too slowly and feel our irritation growing, or someone at home will do something that we'd normally not react to, but for some reason, today, it pushes us into a heightened state of annoyance. We all have these moments, times when we're on edge, when the little things suddenly seem like a big deal, and what's worse is that these moods can sometimes snowball, turning our day—or series of days—into an uncomfortable state where we're difficult to be around. Some of us know people who seem to live in this space for months or even years.

When we find ourselves annoyed over the little things, using today's question, "Just what am I afraid of?" is a helpful way to find out what's really going on. What I've found is that whenever I'm annoyed by someone's behavior, or quick to react to something small, it often means there's a bigger issue going on that I'm afraid of or not dealing with. I'll never forget the first time I made this connection. I was driving to work on a beautiful morning when I suddenly found myself irritable and annoyed by the behavior of other drivers, especially those I felt were driving too slowly. I found myself tailgating for no reason, changing lanes, and speeding to get ahead. In a moment of clarity, I slowed down, took a deep breath, and asked myself, *What are you afraid of?* Instantly, I knew the answer.

The week before, I had gone to the doctor to have her examine a suspicious red bump on my little finger. She didn't like the look of it, so she cut it out and sent it off to be biopsied. She said, not as convincingly as I'd have liked, not to worry about it. I didn't follow her instructions. While driving, I realized my mood had nothing to do with the other drivers—or my job or anything else. Instead, I was afraid of what the lab results might show.

This was an invaluable insight for me, and by understanding the connection between my mood and my fear, I've been able to find ways to restore a sense of calm and peace in my life. These days, whenever I find myself discontented in any way, I pause and ask myself what I'm afraid of because when I think deeply enough, I can invariably trace my discomfort back to a fear. When I find what I'm afraid of, I open myself up to the solution by asking:

- What action or decision can I take to reduce this fear?
- What can I do right now, or who can I share this with who will give me some perspective on it?
- Have I done all I can to find a resolution to this?
- Do I need to let go and let time find the proper solution?

Going through this series of questions always relieves the fear and even gives me a sense of empowerment.

The next time you find yourself unsettled or find that the little things are causing unreasonable, overblown reactions and making you and those around you uncomfortable, ask yourself what you're afraid of. Once you've identified the fear, ask yourself what you can do to deal with it. You'll find that once you identify the true cause, the solutions won't be very far away.

It'll never be all right until it's all right, right now.

Many of us tend to spend a lot of time delaying our happiness. We convince ourselves that we will only be at peace, feel secure, or be truly happy when we finally have enough money in the bank, when we're finally debt free, when we've received the promotion at work, or when we're retired—that's when we'll be able to relax and enjoy things. Or maybe when the kids have moved out, graduated college, and have started a career they like, that's when we will begin living for ourselves again. As many of us have discovered, though, when those things do come to pass, we find that they either didn't give us the security or peace we thought they would, or as is often the case, something else has replaced them and off we go chasing that next thing that is sure to give us those feelings of finally feeling all right.

A wise friend and I were talking about this one afternoon, and as I was describing the next set of circumstances I felt sure was going to give me that level of peace and comfort, he said, "Michael, things are good enough for you to feel that sense of peace right now." He then explained that he, too, used to set conditions on his happiness, and each time he did, he watched those goals get pushed further and further into the future. He said that as he reviewed his past, he saw that happiness and serenity were always available to him; he just couldn't see it because he was so focused on getting something or achieving something else first. Ultimately, he told me I already had everything I needed to feel secure and happy right here, right now, and that if I couldn't see that, then chances are I wouldn't be able to see it in the future either.

Many of us have a similar experience as we rush through life chasing the next thing or condition that we've convinced ourselves is a prerequisite for our happiness. As we do, we pass by the moments that are already filled with everything we need to experience those feelings right now. The ability to enjoy the coolness of a fall morning, or the loving hug of a spouse or child, or the abundant material wealth we already possess can give us the feelings of comfort and security we all long for. All these things are here, right now. Unless or until we accept and appreciate them in this very moment, we will continue to delay our joy until that elusive "someday." Stop right now and look around you. Everything is all right, right now, and that realization is the true start to the peace and happiness you're looking for elsewhere.

"The first recipe for happiness is: avoid too lengthy meditation on the past."

—Andre Maurois

We all have a past. Some of us have happy, secure memories, while others have mixed or conflicting memories that we struggle to reconcile. Others of us have childhoods we wish we could change: parents who were absent emotionally or even borderline abusive. Because our past is so much a part of who we are today, it's natural for us to revisit it, to bring up selected memories of those good or bad times. If our childhoods were less than perfect, we might find ourselves reliving the pain or the neglect we felt and end up wishing it were different or better. We might even feel that somehow we were to blame.

Unfortunately, revisiting hurtful memories from our past (without professional help) rarely helps heal them. I've sat with many people who were tormented by the rearview mirror, who wished earnestly that they had acted differently, but all that time spent there didn't change it. Even the desire to understand that endless question of "why" doesn't give us closure sometimes. I know the pain of a less than ideal past. My father was a lost, resentful, and abusive man. My mother checked out early and spent her time and attention on damage control. I grew up neglected, scared, alone. It took many years for me to discover and recover a sense of self, to realize that my past was just that—my past. Once I detached from it, I realized it didn't have to define my present or my future anymore.

One saying I learned years ago was "It's okay to look at the past; just don't stare." A friend explained to me that there are lessons in my past, and that it was okay to visit it in stages, look at what it has to teach me, and then it's crucial to come back to the present and apply those lessons. The strategy of taking contrary action, a concept we discussed earlier, is a helpful one to apply in regard to the past. For example, I was isolated when I was a kid, discouraged from forming friendships, and taught not to trust people. For years, I followed that bad advice and remained closed off. Now, however, I've learned not to listen to that old conditioning, to act differently from what I learned in the past. Even if I don't "feel like it," I take the opposite action anyway and grow each time I do.

By avoiding lengthy meditation on my past, I've learned the most valuable lesson of all: while I may not have had control over my past, I do have control over my present. What I choose to do today will change who and what I become tomorrow. Moreover, by taking the right actions today, I can create not only a new tomorrow but also a new past: past days, weeks, and months filled with positive, supportive, and healthy decisions that will give me the happiness and peace I felt I had missed out on earlier. I've learned it's never too late to create the life I always wished I could have had.

Formula for failure:
try to please everyone.

O kay, I'll admit it: I used to be a card-carrying member of the people-pleaser club. Many of you might relate. It seemed easier in my family to go along to get along rather than fight to try to get my way (which I didn't get very often). There are problems with becoming a people pleaser, though. First of all, as you grow up and try to keep pleasing people, you'll find that you just can't please them all. Despite how much you give in to someone, someone else won't be happy. Another problem is that as you keep trying to please other people, the most important person—you—is rarely pleased at all. Plus, a bigger problem is created as well.

What happens as we strive to please people is that we lose track of our real selves. Because we go with the flow so often, we can be difficult to relate to and hard to trust emotionally. Other people have difficulty being in a relationship with us because our opinions and moods are contingent on what the group or most dominant member of our family deems right. In my family, my mother was the dominant force, and for years her word was law. To go against it meant a huge battle, many hurt feelings, and always being wrong. It was just easier to go along with her—even when it wasn't what I wanted to do.

After my stepfather died, my mother, who was in her eighties, couldn't drive any longer and needed assistance each week to get to the market, doctors' appointments, and so on. These duties fell primarily on my sister and me as my two older brothers were not available to help. Being the people pleaser I was, I threw myself into the weekly routine, and I was soon exhausted and a bit resentful. When I complained to a friend that I felt trapped, she taught me that my well-being was my responsibility. She told me it was up to me to set and live by healthy boundaries.

As I decided to pull back a bit, I got the expected pushback—especially from my sister. For example, when I reported I wouldn't be available one weekend, both my mom and my sister let me have it. At this point, I had to ask myself which pain was worse: the pain of going along to please everyone and hating myself, or the pain of suffering the wrath of family members as I began to establish some boundaries? And that's when the miracle of this technique began.

After suffering through their displeasure, something surprising happened. As I began taking care of myself, my sister started setting her own boundaries, and my mom found other ways to get her needs met. My mom broke out of her isolation and got better acquainted with a neighbor who was happy to be of service and help drive her around. They even got close and began spending afternoons drinking tea together. Before long, my mom was happier, more independent, and even empowered. As a result, my relationship with her improved.

If you're still a card-carrying member of the people-pleaser club, realize that the one person you're not pleasing very often is yourself. In addition, you may be enabling a dysfunctional relationship or dynamic and denying other people the chance to grow and develop. The way to fix this is by being true to yourself and setting healthier boundaries. The sooner you do, the happier you'll be, and you just may be surprised at how other people become happier, too.

43

Always take the high road.

We will always be involved in situations where there is more than one way to respond. It could be during a dispute or disagreement, or even a seemingly innocuous conversation that takes an unexpected turn. Perhaps someone slights us or makes a thoughtless, snide, or passive-aggressive comment. It could be a situation among neighbors or with coworkers that offers us choices as to how we'll conduct ourselves. Do we stoop down to their level and answer tit for tat and so keep the uncomfortable interactions going, or do we ignore our hurt pride and indignant feelings and take the high road instead? While in the middle of an argument or on the receiving end of a petty comment or aggressive attitude, it can be hard to access our better selves, yet on those occasions when we do, we're always rewarded by the result.

To start with, you'll always feel better when you act with grace and kindness than when you respond pejoratively. When we belittle someone, those negative feelings tend to stay with us. We often obsess over them, not only replaying the hurtful behavior of the other person but also role-playing how we could have retaliated even more. Rehearsing the interaction in this way tends to keep the dispute going, and we're primed to continue the insults or hurt feelings the next time we see or interact with the other person. By taking the high road instead, we free ourselves of this negative energy, and we free the other person as well. In addition, something else usually happens: the other person often responds positively to our kindness. Everyone appreciates thoughtfulness. The quickest way to dissolve a dispute or argument is by simply accepting that other people think and feel differently than you do. It's best to elevate the conversation by treating them respectfully—you know, the way you'd like to be treated. Many long-standing disagreements have been healed by this approach.

Opportunities to take the high road are available to us in more than just face-to-face interactions. I see them in any situation where I have a choice in how I'm going to respond to someone. Emailing is a good example. Oftentimes, we have to reach out to customer service teams to get something corrected. Sometimes the teams either don't fix the problem or they respond with unhelpful solutions. We can then either berate them by sharing our dissatisfaction or we can respectfully communicate by empathizing with how busy they must be and by politely asking again.

Other situations give us choices as to how to act, and each one makes a big impact on others. Do we send a text when someone we know loses a parent or do we send a heartfelt card instead? If someone has surgery or loses a job, or if they are dealing with a difficult family situation, do we check in with them regularly or even suggest getting together for a cup of coffee or tea? While it may seem easier to wait for them to recover or resolve the issue they're going through, extending ourselves represents the higher path and makes the most difference. There are countless opportunities for us to take the high road—cleaning something up for a neighbor rather than complaining about it, helping a coworker rather than ignoring their workload, leaving a table or area clean for the next person. Each time we do, we feel better, and so does the other person.

Ultimately, taking the high road is the easier and better way to go through life. It often takes a lot less energy, leaves everyone feeling much better, and it sets us up for a happier, more peaceful interaction in the future. The next time you have a choice, take the high road and see where it leads you.

H.A.L.T.

There are times when we all feel out of sorts. Nothing much may have changed in the outside world: our jobs, families, homes, etc., may be relatively the same, but our attitude about them can shift. You know how it is. Our spouse may be doing the same things he or she always does, but for some reason, today, this behavior pushes us over the edge. When you find yourself in such a mood, it's helpful to look for an obvious—and likely—cause.

This acronym, H.A.L.T., is a great place to start. It stands for **hun**gry, **a**ngry, **l**onely, **t**ired. What's so powerful about this simple strategy is that these states of being are ones we all experience at one time or another.

Hungry is the first thing I look for in myself, or my wife, because it's very predictable, and its effects are immediately recognizable. Like most of us, I eat three meals a day, and at regular times in the day, so if I miss one, or delay one, or too much time goes by without at least snacking, then the effects are immediate. Whenever I haven't eaten in a while, my energy drops, it's harder to focus, and I find myself getting a little short-tempered. When this happens, I'm quick to ask myself when my last meal was. If I realize I'm hungry, then the quickest way to restore my attitude is to eat. My wife and I often joke halfway through a needed meal and ask, "Has the color come back into the world yet?" It always does once we've taken care of our hunger.

The next thing I ask myself when I find my attitude is a little sharp or curt is whether I'm *angry*. Anger is a tricky emotion because it's one we've been taught to hide. No one likes to be around an angry person, so we often have to swallow our anger, and this can lead to wallowing in it. You can imagine the state that puts us in. Whenever I'm feeling aggressive or quick-tempered, I ask myself if I'm angry about something. In addition, I also find that my anger can be caused by harboring something unrelated to the current situation or person. Either way, once I've found what or who I'm angry at, I can stop taking it out on things or on other people, and instead I can figure out how to resolve it appropriately.

The next one—am I *lonely*?—is a bit harder to diagnose, because sometimes I can be in a group of people and still feel lonely. When this happens, I examine whether I'm engaging with others, whether I'm disclosing what's going on with me, or if I'm not, why not? Connecting with those I'm with, even "faking it until I feel like it," helps a great deal when I'm with others and find myself isolating and not feeling a part of the group. Obviously, if I'm alone, the solution is to reach out to someone or even walk outside and connect with the neighbors. Anything to get outside of myself—texting others, for example—works just as quickly to help restore my attitude.

The last thing to analyze is whether or not I'm *tired*. If I haven't had enough sleep, this is an easy state to diagnose, but it can be hard to honor it and then give myself the extra space I need. Life is still in session, and I'm still expected to pay attention and to perform at work or home, whether I've had enough sleep or not. More common, though, and harder to detect is when I lose energy and focus because I need a break. I often work myself too hard, drive myself to get things done, and keep going until I've exceeded my limits. The key here is to H.A.L.T. and ask myself if I need a break or if whatever I'm working on wouldn't be best accomplished later on when I feel fresher. Recognizing this goes a long way to being both more efficient and improving my attitude.

Ultimately, we can all slip into a difficult mood, and we'll all have times when we're just not feeling like ourselves. Thankfully, the H.A.L.T. checklist is an easy and reliable way to restore us to the selves we'd like to be.

45

"Material success may result in the accumulation of possessions; but only spiritual success will enable you to enjoy them."

—Nido Qubein

We've discussed how many of us are convinced that the path to success, to security, and to eventual happiness is in the accumulation of outside things, and key among those things is the accumulation of money. *If only I could win the lottery, that would solve all my problems,* you might say to yourself. All the longing we have, as well as the worry and unsettledness we feel, would all go away if we just had enough money. So, we all work hard to earn it and to get the things it can buy, and many people do collect them, but what they inevitably report is what we've all heard before: money can't buy happiness. The reason for this is that the ability to enjoy that money or those possessions is dependent on our spiritual development, and until we make that our first priority, we won't find the peace, security, or happiness many of us long for.

You may have heard the saying that we're not human beings having a spiritual experience, we're spiritual beings having a human experience. What this means is that we are not here to feed our material selves; rather, our real purpose is to grow spiritually, to develop our awareness of and appreciation for the higher sides of our nature. These include expanding our capacity for empathy, deepening our relationship with and dependence on our concept of a Higher Power, and truly developing our desire to be guided by our highest calling. Most of us have known moments when we have achieved a temporary state of grace, usually those times when we have acted selflessly, without expecting anything in return. Love offers us the surest path to this feeling as we put another person's well-being and interests ahead of our own. This state is the antithesis of trying to achieve outside success, and when we act in this unselfish and loving way, it's remarkable how our worries, insecurities, and fears evaporate, and we enter the state of security and peace we've been striving for.

We all have the ability to cultivate and feel this way more often, and it all starts by making our spiritual success as important as our material success. Simple changes in your daily routine can have a big impact on your overall feelings of calm and inner peace. Just think about how much time you spend reading about your favorite sports team or the latest article on your phone or how much time you spend on social media. If you consciously devoted some of that time to reading something that fed your spirit instead, like favorite devotional quotes or books that resonate with you, you would expand your spiritual awareness and feed your soul. The wonderful part of this is that your spiritual self grows quickly; it responds immediately to just a little bit of nourishment. The light is easier to feed than the darkness. By changing your mental diet in this way, you will notice yourself being more patient, more contented, and you'll be more likely to help others and give more of yourself. You will be experiencing spiritual success.

As you do, you will find that you'll begin enjoying all the material possessions you already have. You'll need less of them because you'll be filled with the deeper feelings of peace and contentment they could never give you. Then you'll know the truth: everything you've always wanted is already inside of you; you simply have to look within to find it.

46

Expect nothing, accept everything.

I was watching an interview with a famous actor one day, and the interviewer commented on how calm and centered he seemed to be. The interviewer asked what his secret was. The actor said that, over time, he found that the best way to keep a sense of serenity was to truly let go. He said he approached all interactions and situations with the attitude of expecting nothing and accepting everything. He added that despite being rich and famous, he realized he couldn't control people, places, or things, and trying to do so only caused a lot of stress. As such, it was best to give up the illusion of control and just accept everything as it was.

While this is a simple attitude to have, it obviously isn't an easy thing to practice. The good news is that while we may not be able to rid ourselves of all expectations right away, you'll find that just lowering them can pay huge dividends. The first step is being aware of the expectations you have about any situation. Going to the DMV is a great example. Whether to renew your license, change ownership of a vehicle, and so on, examine your expectations, like how much time it will take, how helpful the other person will be, and what you expect the results to be. Based on your previous experience, how likely is it to turn out the way you expect? Next, begin reducing or letting go of them, one by one. Even letting go of some of your expectations will release you from being attached to the result, and this frees you up to observe and accept things as they are and how they turn out. Maybe you brought all the documentation you needed, or you didn't. Maybe the wait was shorter or longer than you allowed time for. Maybe the other person was in a good mood and helpful, or they were having a rough day. Regardless, by releasing your expectations ahead of time, you'll be able to reduce stress and disappointment, and be more present and accepting of the experience—and the result.

Once we stop pushing, manipulating, or wishing things weren't the way they are, we achieve a great freedom and serenity. We come to see that most things are just the way they are supposed to be—even if they aren't the way we'd like them to be. Moving into acceptance in this way disentangles us from the resentments and hurt feelings that can accompany expectations, and it allows us to be more peaceful and forgiving. While you may not be able to practice this all the time, or perfectly, you reap huge benefits by training yourself to expect less and accept more. As you get better at it, watch your stress level go down and your feelings of serenity go up.

47

Fake it till you make it.

This is one of the best strategies I know of for overcoming the fear of trying something new and for breaking out of self-imposed limitations. It works in all areas of life, and the best part of it is that the more you use it, the more comfortable with it you'll become and the more willing you'll be to try it again.

The first time I heard it, I had graduated from college and began looking for work. I was intimidated by the business world and felt much more comfortable in the cloistered halls of academia. I didn't have experience in business, didn't have much of a résumé, and I wasn't sure how to go about getting that first position. That's when someone told me to "fake it till you make it." He told me that if I wanted to be a successful business professional, I first had to look the part. I went out and bought a couple of suits, a shiny pair of shoes, and a briefcase. Next, he told me to scan the classifieds, make the calls, and set up interviews. He said that when I went on interviews, I was to assume the attitude of a confident, eager professional, someone who belonged in the business world. It was scary at first, but eventually I got comfortable in those suits, acclimated to the interviews, and soon enough, I had my first real job. Over the years, I used this same strategy to work my way up the corporate ladder, always assuming the next level, looking and acting as if I belonged—until I did.

New parents use this strategy all the time, although they may not recognize it. There is no college course or degree in becoming a parent. One day your child is born, you bring him or her home, and *boom*—you're a parent! You have no choice at that moment; you have to fake it till you make it, and you do. You learn along the way. You make mistakes, and you get better at it. Then the next one comes, and suddenly, it's easier, you're more confident, and soon you develop your own way of raising kids and being a parent.

This strategy of faking it can also be called "suiting up and showing up." The idea is the same: you decide what it is you want to do, and you show up and begin doing it, confident that if others can do it, you can, too. If you don't know exactly how yet, that's okay—you'll figure it out. The key, though, is to get started.

As I mentioned in the beginning, this strategy can be used for just about anything you're hesitant about trying and can help you make needed changes in your life. Out of shape? No problem. The solution is as simple as getting a gym bag or backpack, sneakers, some workout clothes (or even just a pair of shorts), joining a local gym, and then showing up and getting on a bike or treadmill. And just like that, you are a gym-goer! Do this often enough, and you may even begin taking classes or lifting weights. Continue showing up, and soon your diet may change and after faking it in this way, you'll find yourself in the shape you hope to be in.

The secret to this whole strategy is realizing that you don't have to know how to do something perfectly to at least get started trying. No one has all the skills or knowledge to try something new or to begin doing the things that interest them, and, unfortunately, that often stops them from even attempting it. Because beginning is often the hardest step, it's also the most important one. Given the freedom of faking it at first allows you to see that you can often do a lot more than you think you can. Once you finally get started and actually begin doing it, you'll see that you *can* do it. And that's when faking it becomes making it!

If I'm not the problem, then there is no solution.

This is one of the most valuable life lessons I've ever been given. It's also one of the hardest to fully accept and then to practice. However, once I have humbled myself to truly take in the weight of its wisdom, and once I become willing to apply it to all the areas of my life, I discover a new freedom. I become empowered to make the changes I can to bring me the peace and serenity I seek.

At the heart of this lesson is the simple truth that I have a role in all the situations in my life. It may be an active role or a passive role, an obvious one or a more subtle one. No matter what I'm involved in, though, there is a part I play in the interaction or situation. Furthermore, and most importantly, my part in that situation is the only one I can affect or change. I can rarely change another person, institution, or thing, but I can change my actions, attitudes, or feelings about them. This is why I hold the solution to every problem in my life today.

Examples of this lesson are available in each area of our lives. Interpersonal relationships with family members or with people we work with are the most obvious places to look to. Whenever you get into a disagreement with a spouse, for example, a common tendency is to prove your point or focus on what they're doing wrong. But what about your part? What are you doing to keep the disagreement going? I've heard it said that when you're pointing a finger at someone, three fingers are pointing back at you. Continuing to blame others just keeps us in the problem and leads to resentments and hurt feelings. When you reach this point, resolution seems far away, and sometimes these resentments can turn into long-standing obstacles that can ruin a relationship.

This deadlock can be quickly resolved by simply looking at your part and committing to change what you can. This is often the work we do in therapy. Before I transitioned to business coaching, I worked with a couple who had very different ways of thinking about things and arrived at decisions through very different processes. The husband was more of a spur-of-the-moment thinker, and once he locked onto something, he tended to go after it. The wife, on the other hand, was more of a practical thinker, liked to think things through, and consider all angles before making a decision. The problem they had was that the husband often made decisions, and the wife just went along—harboring and building resentments until she couldn't take it any longer.

When we worked through this issue together, it became clear that neither one of them could change the way the other person thought about things. They could, however, both examine their own part in the disagreement. The wife's part was that she just went along with her husband's decisions without thoroughly voicing her own opinion and opposition. The husband's part was that he took his wife's compliance as complicit acceptance and approval of his decisions. The solution, as it almost always is, was to communicate more clearly and to introduce a new step in their decision-making process: one of openly discussing an issue and taking in each other's point of view before making decisions to move forward. By implementing this solution, the wife no longer felt like a victim, and the husband no longer felt like the bad guy who was always to blame.

Clearly understanding our part in any problem in our lives immediately restores the power we have because our part is the only one we can change. While all the situations or problems we have may not be able to be solved as in the previous example, what we do have power over is how we deal with them, what attitude we choose to take, and what we can change or do differently next time. Once you honestly look at your own role in things, you'll find ways you can change to make them better. In other words, once you find that you're part of the problem, you'll find the solution as well.

49

When one door closes, another opens, but it can be tough in the hallway.

L earning to manage change is a valuable life skill to master. Things change all the time, and there's even a saying for it: The only thing that's constant is change. One thing that makes handling change so difficult is our insistence on things remaining the same—especially when we finally have them right where we want them. One way to overcome our resistance to things changing is to reflect back on all the changes that have occurred that ended up being a good thing. If you think back just a little, I'm sure you can come up with many examples of this: Maybe a change of jobs turned out to be the best thing for you, or a move, or not getting what you thought you wanted at the time. It's wise to make a list of these things and have them handy whenever you find yourself anxious about an impending change.

There's another saying about change: When one door closes, another door opens. While this is often true as well, what gets left out of that saying is the other part—that while you're waiting for that other door to open, it can be tough in the hallway. Nobody likes uncertainty, especially when we're not sure of what's coming next. In addition to referring to your list of changes that turned out better than you thought they would, here are some strategies for dealing with the time you might have to spend in the hallway.

The first thing to remember is where to place your focus. While there are things you can do to influence a situation, ultimately many variables may work in concert to decide a specific outcome. Staying focused on the things you can directly influence will help you remain sane in the hallway. If you've suddenly lost your job, for example, things to focus on might include revising your resume and updating your LinkedIn profile. Next, you'll probably want to reach out to your professional network, let them know you're available, and ask about opportunities they may be aware of. It's also a good idea to make a list of other actions you can take daily to get you in front of the decision-makers who can hire you. Recruiters and career management companies are a good place to start. By staying active and focused on the things you can influence, the hallway won't seem so long or so lonely.

The other thing you can do when you find yourself in the hallway is to focus on taking extra good care of yourself. As mentioned, change and uncertainty can be super stressful, and when you find yourself in the hallway, negativity and fear can creep in. During this period, it's helpful to outline things you can do that will reduce your worry and that will make you feel better about yourself. For instance, sitting around gorging on a pint of ice cream may feel good while you're doing it, but the aftereffects of guilt and a bulging waistline will only add to the stress you feel. Taking the extra time to exercise—either getting back to the gym or spending time outdoors—will not only release a lot of the stress you're feeling, it will help you feel better about yourself as well. Think of all the things you enjoy doing, and if you now have the time to do them (reading a good book works for me), then be thankful you have the time and opportunity available to you. There are many other ways to practice self-care: yoga, a bubble bath, browsing in your favorite store, eating well, meditating, endless options, really. Engaging in these activities will do wonders for your attitude.

The hallway is an inevitable part of change, and some are longer than others. By focusing on the things you can influence, and by protecting and nurturing yourself, the hallway doesn't always have to be so tough. You can and will get to the other door, and now you have some strategies to help you through it.

50

When you're done using it, put the mind down.

The mind is the only tool I know of that never seems to stop working. We use it from the moment we open our eyes, all throughout the day, and even when we go to sleep, it's working in the background, manufacturing dreams, trying to reconcile problems and produce solutions. Sometimes we wake up and intuitively know how to handle a situation, and other times the mind simply takes over where it left off and continues to chew on a problem, working on it, trying different approaches, and offering us options to solve it. Our minds are wondrous instruments, seemingly tireless, but sometimes this incredible computer goes a little too far.

There are times when our minds think so much they tend to take over; they work on a problem endlessly, and they can become obsessed with a person or a problem to the point of making our lives unmanageable. Anyone who has laid his or her head on their pillow knows what it's like to have their minds working, racing, jumping from one subject to the next, or stuck rehashing the same thought, worrying over and over again. While it's great to have our supercomputer available to us all the time, it's also important to be able to put it in sleep mode when we want to.

Eckhart Tolle, in his book *The Power of Now*, describes a way to look at our minds that can give us the perspective we need to do just that. He said the mind is an instrument, a tool, and an important habit to get into is to learn to lay it down after using it. Think of the mind as being like a hammer, for example. When you need to drive a nail into something, you go to the tool drawer, pick up the hammer, use it to do its job, and when you're done, you lay the hammer back down in the drawer. You don't then carry the hammer around with you throughout the day, and you certainly don't take it to bed with you!

He said we need to use the mind like a tool: you pick it up when you need it, use it for a specific task, and when you're done using it, you should lay it down till it's needed again. By getting into the habit of doing this, you will be freed up to practice what he calls "being in the now." By learning to live in the now, you'll discover peace, gratitude, and a deep serenity.

Eckhart Tolle describes many ways to disconnect from the mind and different strategies to practice being present and letting go of the constant chatter and activity of the mind. The first step is to recognize whether or not you've laid your mind down after you've picked it up to do something. Just becoming aware of this gives you a choice of whether to keep using it or laying it back down and getting quiet for a moment. This is the beginning of developing an awareness of who is currently in control: you or your mind.

Today, try laying your mind down after you've used it for a specific activity or problem. Once you do, you'll discover the peace and quiet that are always available in the background, waiting for you every moment. Try it now: put your mind down for a moment, take a deep breath, and listen for the silence.

View everyone you meet as a walking Rorschach test.

I used to be super sensitive to what people thought about me. During any interaction, when they said anything negative or judgmental about me, or if they reacted in a way I didn't want or expect, I took it as a personal affront. I'd roll over in my head what they said, what they meant, and I internalized their comments or judgments and could obsess about them for days, weeks, and even years. I was finally given some perspective on my sensitivity when I learned to interpret other people's reactions as more of a reflection on themselves than on me. This was a big revelation for me, and it all started when I learned about the Rorschach test.

In 1921, the Swiss psychiatrist Hermann Rorschach developed a psychological test using a series of inkblots to understand his patient's personality characteristics and emotional tendencies. He would simply show a patient one of ten inkblot cards with different designs and ask them to describe what they saw. In describing what each inkblot meant to them, people would "project" their inner thought processes, revealing any biases, fears, hopes, and tendencies they had. After analyzing thousands of responses to this test, Rorschach found the inkblots delivered a surprisingly accurate and clear picture of a person's underlying personality.

The idea of interpreting someone's thought processes based on how they react to things has surprising applications in our everyday lives. Once I started looking objectively at how other people processed an event or interaction and how they responded to different people and situations, I found that it often had a lot less to do with who I was or what I'd done than it did with the emotions, preconceived ideas, and conditioned responses they brought to the interaction itself. In other words, everyone reacts differently to the same event, and their reaction often reveals a lot more about them than it does about me. By realizing this, I grew less self-conscious and took things much less personally than I used to.

To test this theory, I once made an innocent political statement and then observed what the reaction was. Some people agreed and they immediately became friendly to me while others grew agitated, argued with me, or visibly distanced themselves from me. All I had done was make a simple comment, and suddenly, what I got back in return revealed to me a lot about a person's beliefs, their upbringing, and the force and depth of their convictions. My statement was indeed like a Rorschach test, and rather than take their responses or reactions personally, I was able to detach and put some space between us. This helped me to become more interested in people, and by understanding them more, I found I could empathize with them.

In addition, I started seeing other people—and especially other events—as a Rorschach test for myself. I became a keen observer of my own reactions to things and to other people, and in this way, I was able to learn more about my own hidden beliefs and tendencies. These days, I'm more introspective, and I'm constantly asking myself how I'm feeling about something and why. Once I'm able to trace my reactions back to where they are coming from, I regain some perspective and become open to viewing situations and people for what they truly are: a mirror that I hold up to myself to learn more about my thoughts, feelings, hopes, and fears. This has been a valuable practice for me, and those people I've shared it with have found it helpful as well. Start treating things like a Rorschach test and see what they begin teaching you about yourself. You might be surprised by what you learn.

52

The worst vice is advice.

W e all have opinions, and some of us like to share them a bit too freely. I know there have been times when my own MBA in unsolicited advice has done more harm than good, and I've counted myself among the group of people who can barely contain themselves as they wait for their turn to speak. Let's face it, we all have a lot to say, and we're quick to share our advice as to what we think others should do or how they should act. We try to be helpful, and we're quick to offer advice and direction about how others should handle a certain situation or how they ought to make changes in their lives. It doesn't matter whether we are living the particular way we're suggesting, and it also doesn't matter, in some cases, whether we've even tried the advice out ourselves; if we feel you are stuck, or your life isn't going the way we think it should, then here's the advice on how to change it. There are many problems that come with unsolicited advice, a few being that people usually aren't that receptive to receiving it, and in some cases, they can even come to resent it.

People who think they have the right answers also think they have the solutions to not only yours but to all people's or societies' problems as well. We all know of people who can tell you how to solve everything from global warming to dealing with your teenagers, regardless of whether they're recycling or have children. (I'm reminded here of a saying I once heard: "Take my advice—I'm not using it!") What's especially frustrating is when they share their opinions and advice without you even asking for them. As soon as you mention a problem or an upcoming decision you're contemplating, out comes the advice. As they tell you that you should change this or that, or that you shouldn't be doing this or the other thing to begin with, what they fail to see is their implication that the way you're doing things now, or the way you think about things, is completely wrong. Even if they are genuinely trying to be helpful, the net effect of most advice like this isn't positive and can often leave us feeling worse than before we brought up our problem or situation to begin with.

What people fail to realize is that sometimes what we want more than anything is understanding and acceptance rather than advice. Oftentimes, it's important for us to voice our doubts, our indecision, and the obstacles we face and that what we're looking for isn't a quick fix or suggestion but rather, someone who cares and is there to listen and accept us for who we are. These are the best kinds of friends, as we know, and if we then ask for advice, these caring friends know the number-one rule that classifies all "good advice": advice that is based on experience. Once, a friend was struggling in his relationship with his wife, both insisting that they were right, and neither one being willing to admit fault. He asked me what he should do, and I shared my experience when that comes up in my own marriage.

I simply told him how, when we're butting heads, I found it best to humble myself, carefully consider my wife's needs, and try to put them before my own. Over time, I've found that almost always works out for the best. When you share what happened to you, you are identifying with the other person, and by sharing what happened next, you're providing real-life experience that they can then consider applying to their own situations and lives. This is how advice is transformed into a solution, and that is what we are all ultimately looking for whenever we share a problem. So the next time you have the urge to give your opinion, consider any experience you have first, and share that instead.

53

"Life starts all over again when it gets crisp in the fall."

—F. Scott Fitzgerald

There is so much I love about this quote, and there are so many meanings to take from it, if you just spend a bit of time with it. To start with, the fall is often people's favorite season for all sorts of reasons. Summer's heat releases its grip and cooler temperatures turn the air friendly and inviting again. The world is painted with pleasant hues as leaves turn yellow, orange, and red. The quality of light softens and dims as the days grow shorter. In many countries, pumpkin is the flavor of October, and here in the States we enjoy pumpkin lattes, baked goods, ice cream, and just about every other pumpkin-flavored item you can imagine. Of course, the fall is also the gateway to the most wonderful time of the year, the holidays, and all the joy that brings.

When I begin thinking of fall and life starting all over again, I also think of the coming spring just six months away. Soon after the leaves fall and the holidays pass by, even during winter, if you look closely enough, you can see the new buds on the trees, the shoots of the peonies and other life emerging again, readying themselves for another cycle of life. Spring, as we know, is a new beginning, a vibrant one few of us miss, a season where the days extend themselves, and we drink in the sunshine just like the new leaves do. If we pay attention to this recurring series of rebirths, we begin to appreciate the miracle of life and our place within it.

That's what F. Scott Fitzgerald's quote draws my attention to: the temporal and fleeting, and ultimately precious, nature of the seasons and all of life. So often we miss the magic of the seasons as we plow through each day, our heads down, charging toward what we deem important at the time. I certainly did that much of my life, and each time a new season arrived, I complained that time was moving too fast. December already? Time to make my New Year's resolutions and put my head back down to try to accomplish what I thought was important while the new seasons rushed by. Then I read today's quote, "Life starts all over again when it gets crisp in the fall."

What I've learned to do these days is stop and ask myself what the date is, what season I'm a part of at the moment. Right now, it's July 10, and summer is in full bloom. The trees are heavy with green, and the sun and humidity are in charge. When I go into my garden, the bumblebees are busy, and the dragonflies are beautiful as they delicately flitter and bounce over the front doorstep. By becoming aware of which season I'm a part of, I'm able to somehow slow down time's inexorable march, and for the moment, I'm able to find a peace and comfort I can't get elsewhere. It's a rich and meaningful experience, and it's available to us all, all the time, if we slow down and look around us.

As you read this, what season are you in today? What stage are the trees in and have their buds bloomed yet? What color are their leaves? As you center yourself in the miracle of life, know that whatever challenge you may be facing will change and pass, just like the seasons themselves. Life will renew itself and will renew you in the process. Your only real job is to be aware of that process, to be thankful to be a part of it, and to greet each renewal with gratitude. When you think about it this way, life is pretty simple. It's quite wondrous, too.

54

"We are continually faced with great opportunities brilliantly disguised as unsolvable problems."

—Margaret Mead

If we all gave up when faced with what seemed like unsolvable problems, we wouldn't have made much progress as a species. On a broad scale, we wouldn't have persevered and solved the problems of irrigating crops and so discovered agriculture. We would have given up on the numerous problems with containing the power of steam and turning it into the mighty force it became in driving the Industrial Revolution. Further examples include discovering germ theory and thus penicillin; solving the flight problem and eventually going from Kitty Hawk in North Carolina (site of the Wright Brothers' first flight) to landing on the moon a mere sixty-six years later—a task fraught with seemingly unsolvable problems and deemed impossible by many. Looking back at humankind's great opportunities brilliantly disguised as unsolvable problems, what we see is a history of courageous, inventive, and persistent people who capitalized on them for the betterment of us all.

But it wasn't always easy fighting through the established beliefs and prejudices that stood in the way of this progress. Out of this maze of obstacles, perhaps the biggest challenge is to *think outside the box* as it were, and to become open enough, curious and courageous enough to go against what the majority of people think is right and possible. It has been said that truth passes through three stages. First, it is ridiculed. Second, it is violently opposed. Third, it is accepted as being self-evident. Having the conviction to go through the first two phases is what it takes for those with vision to transcend things as they are and make them into what they can become.

This is the way it is for all of us. We all have desires, dreams, and goals that speak to us, that paint the picture of a better possible life or life experience. To reach this better place, we also face resistance from what others believe is not possible or appropriate for us. Pressure from family, the accepted norms, from friends or social groups can all affect and challenge our beliefs and goals. Should we go back to school and get that degree for a chance at a better or different job? Should we change careers? Start that business? Move to a different city or country? In the face of these decisions there will be resistance from others who are adamant that things won't work out, who will point to all the unsolvable problems, and even call us crazy for trying.

I remember when my wife and I were considering moving from Los Angeles to the other side of the country, North Carolina, where we had only visited once. I'd lived in Los Angeles my entire life, and it's where many people are trying to move to. When I told my doctor this, he scoffed at the idea and told us if we sold our home but then decided to move back, we'd never be able to afford to buy back into the L.A. market. This was definitely a risk, we knew, but we also knew we had to try. It turned out to be a huge change for us, but the adjustment was immediate, and we've never been happier with our decision.

This leads to the point of today's saying: If you have a dream or a vision, it will inevitably come with doubt, with what seems to be unsolvable problems, and you may even have to face some opposition at first. But there is a reason you have that desire. There is a truth in you that will be right for you, despite what others think. At some point, if you follow your dream or intuition, you'll uncover the great opportunity that spoke to you in the first place. And the accomplishment of your goal will soon become self-evident to all those who at first doubted you.

55

Start a journal.

Writing in a journal each morning has been one of the most important self-awareness tools I've ever discovered. I learned about the concept of morning pages from the wonderful book *The Artist's Way* by Julia Cameron. As part of her twelve-week program for discovering and feeding the artist within, she recommends dedicating time in the morning to writing three pages of whatever is in your head. She offers a few guidelines to get you started, and I've since expanded on them so they fit my schedule and creative moods.

To start with, any kind of notebook will work, the only prerequisite is that it feels right to you. Large, small, college-ruled, blank, it's completely your choice. Have some fun browsing a stationery store or your local pharmacy, or just grab a notebook or legal pad you may already own. The point, though, is not to use a computer. Use pen, pencil, colored pens, or even crayons—whatever feels right that day. Writing by hand is the key.

Next, Julia suggests you write three pages, which was daunting at first. Three full pages in a college-ruled notebook? (That's my choice for a journal.) I don't have that much to say! When I first started it was challenging to fill those three pages, and once again Julia offered a helpful suggestion. At those times when you don't feel you have anything to write, then write that. Many of my journal entries begin with "I'm totally blank today! Nothing is going on, and this is stupid—a complete waste of time. *Yada, yada, yada . . .* " I'll sometimes carry on in that vein for a page or more until something comes up—and it always does.

That's why the suggestion for three pages has been so helpful. What I repeatedly find is that the first page and a half is filled with mundane stuff: things I've got to do, random thoughts, and even negative or fearful thoughts. When I persevere, however, something happens halfway through. I go deeper, and the deeper I go, the more hopeful, positive, and empowered I become. It's almost as if there is a layer of negativity that weighs down my inner joy, but once I push through it, I release my inner self. And that inner self is always happy, ready to reveal my true purpose, my hopes, and dreams. It's a wonderful experience that sets me up to have a focused and purposeful day.

A quick note on when to journal. As I'd mentioned earlier, Julia calls these *morning pages* and suggests writing them as early as possible. "By spilling out of bed and straight onto the page every morning, you learn to evade the Censor"—and you gain access to your subconscious. I write mine with my coffee each morning. I understand not everyone's schedule will allow that, and I've had to make many adjustments over the years to get mine in, but I always find it's worth it. I've woken up an hour early to write them before the household awakens or I've arrived at work forty-five minutes early and found a quiet conference room in which to write them. Many coffee shops have also served as journaling stations. I've even journaled at night and found it helpful to empty my mind onto the page, especially if I'm preoccupied or worried about something. Getting my concerns down in my journal has given me the peace of mind to finally relax and get some much-needed sleep.

A couple of final notes: These are *your* pages. Keep them private so you can be as open and honest as possible. Also, this isn't a diary—you never have to reread them if you don't want to. In addition, be as creative as you want. I happen to like stickers and use a variety of them to decorate my pages. I also like to use different color pens depending on my mood for the day. Have some fun and let your creative self, your real self, celebrate *you*. The real magic of journaling is letting the child within express him- or herself, and we all know how free, hopeful, and innocent children are. Your inner child is just waiting to express itself. Start your journal this week and let yourself dream again!

Listen like you
don't have an opinion.

Little kids can teach us a lot about listening. Sure, they ask a lot of questions, but have you noticed how they take everything in and consider it deeply? You can see their little minds processing your answers, storing them, comparing them with what they know and what they don't know. They ask innocently with no other agenda than to learn. Sometimes they seem to stare off into space as you talk, but you know they are listening in a way you may have forgotten, in a deeply curious way, hungry to learn and rack up all your knowledge of the world. People even say children are like sponges— they are aware of everything and soak it all in.

By the time kids become teenagers, they learn to listen differently. Around thirteen on, kids have learned everything from you they need to know, and now they have opinions—lots of them. However, have you ever watched them with their friends? They are still listening carefully, only the source of their information has changed. Now they take their cues from their peers, and they are keenly aware and interested in learning from them. At some point, though, we all become comfortable with ourselves; we've figured the world out, and we change how we listen. For the most part, we prefer to talk, to add information to a conversation, to share our opinion and offer advice. When we become parents, this tendency to teach and share our knowledge comes in handy, but it can have its drawbacks as well.

One drawback is that when we're teaching and talking, we're usually busy thinking about what we're going to say next, and so we stop listening. Truly listening. And when we stop listening, we stop learning and growing. We see this most often when in a group of people or even one-on-one. At these times, we're usually busy comparing what others are saying to our opinion of things, and so we're not really present. An invaluable skill to reacquire is the ability to listen like a child again, to be open and curious. By trying to listen more, we can gain a real understanding of the other person's point of view or understand an issue better or even learn more about a particular religion or custom. And it all starts by learning to listen as if you didn't have an opinion.

To get good at this, you can take a few tips from how children do it. To start with, when speaking with another person, rather than be quick to offer your opinion, do what children do: ask questions. Whenever you find you want to argue with a point or give your side of something, ask another question instead. Then, like a child, truly take the answers in. Really listen. Next, observe the body language of the other person. As they speak, do they use their hands? How animated are they? Do they speed up? What is their pace and tone? The way someone says something reveals a lot about them, about what they believe and how important things are to them. By listening as if you don't have an opinion, you'll be less likely to feel the need to defend or argue with another's point of view. And this is the whole key. Allowing someone to truly express themselves, without judgment, is one of the greatest gifts you can give a person. It is the gateway to true understanding and acceptance. Imagine the peace we'd have in the world if we all did this. While the whole world might not be ready to listen yet, you can begin listening more, and you can start the next time someone starts talking.

What other people think of me is none of my business.

I think many of us are raised to please others. As children, we're taught to behave, to make our parents happy, and to do things for the approval of others. In our middle school years, being accepted is crucially important for our young, evolving sense of self, and being included in the "right" crowd can mean everything to us. Social media has exacerbated our need for approval, for "likes," and for validation. Counting the comments or views or number of friends we have can become the criteria we use to measure our self-esteem. Other people's opinion of us can exert an inordinate amount of influence on our moods, our sense of self, and our very happiness.

Years ago, when I was much younger and struggling with the issue of pleasing others, my therapist said something earth-shattering to me at the time. She told me that what other people thought of me was none of my business. She explained that once I was able to establish a solid grounding of what I felt was right for me, across all areas of my life, and once I started honoring and living by my truth, as she called it, then I wouldn't need the outer validation I was so desperately seeking. She told me that other people's opinions were just that—their opinions. As long as I allowed what other people thought of me to define or influence my happiness, I wouldn't be able to find peace of mind.

As I struggled to disconnect from other people's opinions, I sometimes found I still dwelled on certain people, family members especially. Those long-standing relationships, and their ingrained opinions of me (which had unconsciously become my own), were hard to detach from. My therapist told me that at those times I was dwelling on what they thought of me, I was allowing them to live rent free in my head. I liked that saying a lot, and it helped me as I sought ways to evict them. For a while, I had to limit the time I spent with them so I could establish my own ideas, get clear on my own opinions, and come to my own unique point of view.

One thing that helped with this was when I was ordering from a fast-food Mexican restaurant, in a mall, of all places. On the counter was a brochure for a dating service, and inside they listed a twenty-question survey. They recommended you use it to determine if a person you had begun dating was compatible for you long term. It started with larger questions like identifying your religious or spiritual beliefs, and your political leanings, your opinions on civil rights, etc. Then it drilled down to what you preferred to do with your free time, and what you choose to spend money on, your attitudes about debt, and other financial matters. It was eye-opening for me as I'd never really considered all these issues in depth before. This was the launching point for me, and together with my therapist, I was not only able to identify my clear feelings and preferences for both the large and small issues in my life, but in the process, I became clear on who I was and what I stood for. More importantly I accepted that my opinions were right for me, despite what my family, friends, or others thought of me.

These days, I continue to test, build, clarify, and strengthen my sense of self. While there are still differences between the people I run into, each time I accept those differences, I feel more confident and surer about myself and what's right for me. My job, I realize, is what Shakespeare said so long ago: "This above all else: to thine own self be true." This is much easier to do when I remember that what other people think of me is truly none of my business.

58

Transform your interactions: practice courtesy and kindness.

I n today's world of communicating through texting, memes, and hashtags, we've lost the warmth and underlying decency that make our everyday interactions enjoyable and respectful. Though we're sometimes not aware of our tone and demeanor, other people do feel its impact, and they react to it as well. A few years back, my wife and I were on vacation in Venice, Italy, and we were having trouble navigating our way back to St. Mark's Square. I was a little harried, and I approached a local who was sitting by a fountain. Abruptly, I asked, "Where is St. Mark's Square?"

He looked up at me, not smiling, shrugged his shoulders, and said, "I don't know."

I knew he did, so I said, "Sure you do. How do I get there?"

He paused, stared at me, and said, "If you're going to ask me like that, then I don't know."

At this point, I stopped to consider what he meant, and it occurred to me that I was being another rude tourist. In that instant, I knew what was wrong—and I knew how to correct it. "Let's start this again, okay?" I then walked away, turned, and approached him again. I said, "Good afternoon, how are you?"

His face brightened, and we exchanged pleasantries for a few minutes, and then I asked politely for the directions to St. Mark's

Square. He not only showed me which path to take, but he carefully explained where to turn and what to look for along the way. When he was done, he shook my hand and wished me a good trip.

I still think back to that interaction, and it reminds me of how important it is to greet and treat others the way I'd like to be treated. The easiest way to do this is to remember to be courteous and kind toward others. Throughout our day, we have many opportunities to practice this, and the people in service positions—whether they answer phones as customer service reps or in stores—offer us endless chances to practice being kind and interested in others. A good habit to develop whenever you have to call a service center of any kind—from your cell phone provider to the cable company to your health-insurance agent—is to make note of the person's name and ask how their day is going. They take hundreds of calls a day, usually from unhappy customers, and when you open the call with kindness in your voice, it's nice listening to their tone instantly brighten and change. For the most part, they become much more willing to help you, and your interaction almost always ends better for you both.

Being understanding and aware of what someone else is dealing with also goes a long way to creating a smoother and more pleasant experience. I was at Best Buy recently to return an item. There was just one woman behind the counter dealing with an unhappy couple, and there were three of us in line waiting for her. By the time it was my turn, she was ready for another fight, so I opened by saying, "Wow, you're busy today! Looks like a tough day so far."

She immediately looked up, took a big breath, and said, "Yeah, I'm all alone here, and it's already been a long day." Having overheard her tell the person in front of me that you can only return an opened item during the first fourteen days if you have the receipt, I offered her my receipt and my item and said, "I'll make this easy on you. . . ." By the time we finished the interaction, she offered me the first smile I had seen from her, and she wished me a good day. It didn't take much to have a positive effect on another person, and I left the store with a smile as well.

If you want to transform your interactions with other people, and therefore your day-to-day experience, simply consider what other people might be going through, and be kind to them. Saying please and thank you still mean a lot, and by taking the time to truly connect with someone, asking them how they are doing, or taking a moment to empathize with them, you'll be able to brighten someone else's day—and yours, too.

Worry is a terrible waste of the imagination.

O ur minds are incredible creations. The complexity of our neural networks is astounding, estimated at 100 billion neurons making up over 100 trillion neural connections, all capable of working together to create possibilities for thought in nearly infinite combinations. We have access to this powerhouse literally at our fingertips, and we can access, control, and direct its magnificent power simply by choosing what to focus on. We can transport ourselves to the top of Mt. Everest in our minds, and we can feel the freezing wind whipping through our gloves. We can instantly recall one of thousands of memories and relive the joy or pain of a long-ago event as if it happened just moments ago. We can also dream of a better tomorrow or fear for the worst, and either scenario can feel real for us. We can live in joyful anticipation or wallow in deep dread. All this is happening right between our ears, and we all have the ability to direct these thoughts, these images and emotions, simply by choosing the things we dwell on.

It's also been estimated that despite having a near endless choice of what to think and how to use this supercomputer of a brain, the average person accesses less than 1 percent of its capacity. Eighty percent of the thoughts we dwell on are the same thoughts we had yesterday and the day before that. It seems many of us waste a lot of energy, thought, and imagination dreading what might happen or worrying about a familiar set of problems. Despite the amazing power of our mind to conjure up possibilities or evoke feelings of a better future, we tend to use it in the wrong way, imagining outcomes we don't want.

When we dedicate time and thought to worry, we are, in essence, telling our minds to seek out evidence to validate our fears. Someone once said that worrying is praying for what you don't want to happen, and it's interesting how we often find the proof we're looking for. If we wake up with the thought that it's Monday, and that Mondays are always long and hard, we begin collecting the evidence to support that: we focus on how slow the commute is, how the workload is onerous today, and so on. This works with all other scenarios we worry about as well. Life truly is a self-fulfilling prophesy in that way, and our self-talk is always there to confirm it. "See?" it tells us. "I told you that would happen! Happens every time, doesn't it?" Self-talk like this perpetuates negative ways of thinking and contributes to unproductive habits of thought. Fortunately, there is a better way.

You can change your thinking anytime you like. Once you begin cultivating more positive thoughts and regularly imagining things working out, you'll begin looking for and finding the evidence to support it. Here are a couple of tips to begin: The first step is to become aware of your thoughts and tendencies. Begin listening to your constant stream of self-talk, and when you catch yourself saying something negative, stop and ask yourself what would be a better, more empowering alternative thought or statement. Then, when you find yourself thinking negatively again, switch out that thought for the more empowering one. Next, be proactive by imagining positive outcomes rather than negative ones. If you're job hunting, for example, imagine how you'll feel once you land the right one. Paint these positive emotions in your subconscious and feel them wash through your neural network until you smile to yourself. It feels good having that job you want, doesn't it?

There are many books, audiobooks, YouTube videos, and more on using your imagination in a more positive way, and I encourage you to spend some of your free time learning how to use it more constructively. Remember, you have the power to change your thoughts, and when you do, you change your life.

60

If you're struggling to make a decision involving others, do the right thing.

We've all been there: you pull up to a four-way stop sign, and you know the car on your right is supposed to have the right of way, but they arrived there a second or two after you did. So, is it your turn or theirs? When we're in a hurry, it's easy to justify that it's our turn, but we fail to realize the other driver may be thinking the same thing. Because they are on our right, they go . . . and we go, and, well, you know what happens next.

Contrast this with those times you're calmer and not in such a hurry. Suddenly, there is no struggle to decide if you have the right to go next; instead, fair play, common decency, and a sense of doing the right thing immediately take over, and you even wave for the driver on your right to go first. You can probably imagine the grateful feelings the other driver has as they nod a thank-you to you as they drive away. Feels much better, doesn't it?

We are all faced with making decisions in our lives, and most of them don't involve much debate. Others, though, are harder to make, and there are times when we struggle with what to do. Some things might seem petty, like whose turn it is to take out the trash, while others might be more nuanced, like who should claim credit at work involving a joint project. Other decisions are weightier and can include a history of feelings, like whose turn it is to look after an ailing parent or grandparent. While all of these situations may be different, they all have one thing in common: the right choice is always clear.

By the right choice, I mean doing the right thing. While it may not be your turn to do something, or while technically you deserve the credit for something as well as the other person, the right thing almost always involves putting your ego aside and doing what needs to be done, or what is best for the other person who needs your help. You always know what the right thing is because the moment you do it, you feel better. It feels right. This always happens so long as you can release your sense of entitlement or resentment or self-interest. Once you look at it in this way, doing the right thing soon becomes your first choice.

Getting into the habit of automatically doing the right thing is liberating. As soon as I look for the best actions I can take in any situation, like making it my default to do things around the house that need to be done, my mind gets quiet and calm as it's no longer keeping score on whose turn it was, and I stop blaming others. The other consequence is that my wife becomes more appreciative of the little things I'm doing to help. We get along better, and there is more peace at home. The same thing happens at work or when in social situations or at athletic events. Volunteering to break down the nets at a soccer game or collect the balls just makes everything easier and better for everyone.

These days, whenever you're struggling with a decision that involves others, ask yourself what the right thing to do is, and then go ahead and do it. It's one of the quickest ways to invite peace and the good feelings of others into your life.

"How we spend our days is, of course, how we spend our lives."

—Annie Dillard

There is a tendency some of us have to put off doing the things we enjoy until we get our lives "just right." A common thought is that once the kids move out or once we attain a senior position at work or—perhaps the most common of all—once we retire and have all our time to ourselves, that's when we'll finally take up that hobby, read all those books, spend more time traveling, etc. Unfortunately, we've all heard stories (or even known people directly) who passed away before that retirement or "someday" came. When I read today's quote, it really stopped me and made me think about how I spend my days. I wondered how I could incorporate more of the life I hoped to live in the future into my days right now.

The first challenge many of us have is that we're all quite busy. Families, earning a living, obligations, daily chores—the list goes on. Carving out some time each day can seem impossible at first, but it can be done if you start small. The first thing to do is to identify the little things you enjoy and that have meaning to you. I like to break these down into three categories: things I can work into my life on a daily basis, then weekly, and then monthly or quarterly.

The daily items usually take the least amount of time, and they can be restorative, relaxing, and meaningful if we make time for them. The British stop everything at four o'clock each afternoon for teatime. Many people on this side of the Atlantic have discovered this tradition, too. Having that "cuppa" each day can be a cherished time to slow down for a few minutes and enjoy the here and now. Getting into the habit of taking a walk each day—preferably at the same time, like after dinner or during your lunch break at work—provides time to detach from responsibilities and get in those all-important steps. It also gives you a chance to enjoy the world around you. Listening to music, whether you are working at your desk or doing housework or yardwork, can give you an emotional lift. I like to put in my Air-Pods and listen to favorite songs as I do my chores outside. Even a few minutes spent listening to music like this adds so much pleasure. Meditating for five minutes has a surprising power to ground you, as does reading something spiritual at night instead of checking your smartphone for the fiftieth time.

Weekly events usually take a bit more time, and many of them are best carried out in the evenings or on the weekends. Establishing a routine of a few days at the gym each week (if possible), or joining a group of people for a regular weekly activity, such as playing mah-jongg, pickleball, bowling, or a card group, provides wonderful opportunities for socializing. In addition, it gives you something to look forward to. Date nights are popular, and they don't need to be extravagant and expensive. Lately, my wife and I have started the habit of seeing a movie on $5 Tuesdays when the crowds are lighter. It's fun to watch a new release, grab a bag of popcorn and a soda, and sit back and relax. Think about what you enjoy doing—or what you used to enjoy that you stopped doing. Ask yourself how you can work that back into your life on a regular basis.

Monthly or quarterly, it's very exciting to go on a trip. Even a short weekend away or a staycation in your hometown can give you something to look forward to. Anticipation is half the fun of traveling, and once you decide on a trip—with or without the kids—put it on the calendar and begin planning all the things you're going to do; you'll find that your days are suddenly colored by the upcoming break in your routine. Even planning a day trip with the kids to visit a pumpkin patch in the fall or a lavender farm in the summer can give everyone a much-needed change of pace.

As you think of all the enjoyable and meaningful things you can add to your days and weeks, you'll soon find that you are living more of the life you may have been putting off for a later date. I purposefully plan my days now with the intention of adding bits of joy and pleasurable activities as often as I can. Even a quick couple of games of dominos after a meal fill our house with laughter and fun. It's important to do this because how we spend our days is, of course, how we spend our lives.

Anger is one letter away from danger.

Life is filled with annoyances, long-standing hurts and disagreements, and different opinions and viewpoints. Occasionally, we bump up against people and get pushed to a breaking point. It might start with something as simple as the postman not taking the package we left out, a neighbor's dog barking all night, or maybe it's a phone call from a family member that sets us off. At some point, we can lose our composure and slide from annoyance into full-blown anger. When that happens, danger may not be far behind us.

Road rage is a good example of this. We have all experienced other drivers acting irresponsibly—weaving in and out of traffic, tailgating dangerously, or speeding recklessly—and I learned long ago that the safest and sanest thing to do is pull over into a slower lane and let those crazy drivers pass; I'd rather have them way in front of me than behind me. Sometimes, I've even seen other driver's anger turn dangerous, and I've watched in horror as they speed after those reckless drivers and have seen some high-speed chases end in disaster.

Many other things besides an unsafe or obnoxious driver can also trigger us into a state of danger as well. Long-standing disagreements with coworkers or family members often push us to do things we later regret, as well as differing opinions over a political view or religious affiliation or some people's choices in life. People are highly polarized these days, and some situations can move us to anger and spark dangerous emotional states, or even physical reprisals. It is often a very small leap from anger to danger—one letter—and by recognizing this, we can take steps to avoid some ugly consequences.

The first thing to remember is that when we get angry, we're often already in a dangerous place emotionally. We're not thinking clearly or rationally, and the best thing to do is to "pull over" and let the anger pass. We can literally walk away (if possible) and give ourselves some space to collect our thoughts, or we can agree to disagree to avoid escalating an argument or difference of opinion. One of my favorite techniques when dealing with someone whose anger is rising is to simply lower my voice and say, "You know, you may be right." This instantly takes the steam out of any argument or disagreement and gives both of us the chance to settle down.

Keeping our anger from turning into danger is easier if you have these kinds of strategies in place ahead of time. My wife and I have outlined some situations that cause stress and get us worked up, and we've identified some actions to take and some key words we can use to help us step back and de-escalate a situation. Whether it's a neighbor's annoying behavior, or someone pushing in line in front of us, we simply say, "This is inconsequential, let's let it go." This immediately restores our perspective and calms us down.

Today, think about the situations that tend to trigger you, and then plan some solutions for dealing with them in advance. If you do, you may be able to stop your anger from boiling over into danger, and that will save you a lot of trouble in the future.

63

You can always start your day over.

Have you ever had one of those days when something doesn't go right? Maybe you wake up and immediately stub your toe, or find that the sprinkler in your backyard is leaking, or discover that the Internet is out again on a day that you are working from home and have a video conference. From there, it all seems to go downhill. It's as if the universe has decided it's just not your day today, and you begin looking for the next thing to go wrong, looking for more evidence of why today is going to be a bad day. When you start looking for that evidence, isn't it interesting that you often find it? You get extra work from a coworker, someone eats the leftovers you were looking forward to, and that forgotten bill arrives after you've already spent that month's money. When we're in a negative mindset, things can snowball quickly, and once we're on the lookout for the other shoe to drop, as the saying goes, it can be a long day, indeed.

Wouldn't it be nice to be able to go back to the morning and start your day again? While you can't physically go back in time and do that, you can do something just as effective: you can start your day over from right where you are at this moment. It's called a "reset," and it's what professional athletes are taught to do when something bad happens so they can avoid getting into a negative mindset that can ruin the rest of their game. It works like this: In tennis, for example, if a player makes a bad shot or two, their tendency is to be disappointed, to question their ability, and to get down on themselves. This can lead to self-defeating thoughts like *Today isn't my day*, or *I'm not as good as the other player*, or *I'm probably going to lose today*, and so on. While coaches want the player to begin thinking positively, they know it's often hard to go from negative thinking to positive thinking. That's when the concept of the reset comes in: high-performance coaches teach athletes that they must establish a neutral mindset first.

To do this, when a shot doesn't go well or when the other player hits a winner, they suggest the player acknowledge what just happened by saying to themselves, *That's okay*, and then taking a breath, and accepting it objectively and without judgment. Doing so is the quickest way to get to a neutral mindset. After that, coaches teach the player to look for solutions next. *What just happened?* is the next question a player can use to determine what went wrong, and then asking, *Now what?* instantly moves the player into a positive mindset where they can adjust their play or shot selection to be more effective on the very next play. This quick progression from negative to neutral to positive is the best way to keep from dwelling on the negative, and it can be very useful for us in starting our days over as well.

If you find your day isn't going the way it should—or the way you'd like it to—rather than stay negative and look for evidence to support that, simply say, *That's okay*, and get back to neutral. Next, ask yourself, *What just happened?* and acknowledge that maybe you hit a bump in the road. Then, ask yourself, *Now what?* and move on to the solution: call the irrigation company and set a repair appointment; restart your Internet or get some help; and then move on to the precious day you still have in front of you. You really can start your day over again. You can do it as many times in a day as is necessary, and you can do it at any time of the day. Remember, every day is a present, and always focus on untying the ribbons.

64

How to overcome a resentment.

Resentment is a corrosive emotional state that hurts you a lot more than the person, organization, or institution that you hold on to that opened you up to it. There is a common saying that describes this: "Resentment is like taking poison and waiting for the other person to die." Harboring resentment infects us emotionally, spiritually, and even physically, and rolling over what a person or even a country has done to us can negatively affect our lives. My father was a Pole who fled Warsaw and fought in the Polish squadron of the R.A.F. during World War II. Despite promises from both Britain and the United States to restore Polish sovereignty, they stood by as Russia took control of his country after the war. He never overcame this betrayal, was never able to return home to see his loved ones, and his resentment over this ruined the years he had left and affected our family in devastating ways. Finding a way to let go of the resentment we feel in our own lives can be an immensely healing and freeing experience.

I learned the following technique from a spiritual teacher more than twenty years ago, and I've found it to be very effective if you're willing to sincerely try it. It's simple enough, and there are some guidelines to make sure you get the most out of it. Here's what it is: for two weeks, you "treat" the person you resent by getting quiet each day, thinking about them and wishing them everything they want, and by sending them nothing but positive thoughts. If you pray, then praying for them for two weeks is ideal. The whole point of the treatment is that instead of resenting them or thinking about how they hurt you, you instead send them nothing but unconditional acceptance and even love.

Now here are some helpful hints: First, if you don't know what they want or what would make them happy, then pray for them to get all the things *you* want. Health, contentment, happiness, money, recognition—any and all of the things that would make your life better, wish for the other person as well. If you are having trouble with this, then the next tip might help: it doesn't matter whether you actually feel or mean these things or not. I know that might sound counterintuitive, but trust me, it works. What I find is that while I may not believe it at first, something happens midway through or toward the end of the two-week trial. Either I come to mean it, or it just doesn't matter to me whether I believe it or not. What I discover is that I've moved from resentment to a detached acceptance, and the treatment has worked. Other times, I find that it works so well that I not only release the resentment I had, I come to truly wish the other person well. That's a powerful healing.

Like all spiritual treatments, this works if you're simply willing to give it a fair trial. There is something powerful about love and acceptance, and just by practicing it (rather than hatred and resentment), you yourself are moved and changed by it. Since we all have opportunities to try this, I highly recommend you consider using it the next time you feel resentment poisoning your life. Imagine how much better you'll feel when you get the same relief other people do who use this spiritual practice regularly to invite more love and peace into their lives.

65

Don't ruin an apology
with an excuse.

Nobody is perfect. On any given day, we're going to make mistakes, act on old programming, and make selfish or short-sighted decisions. We're going to give in to fear or greed or self-centeredness and generally show a side of ourselves we're not very proud of at the time. While we have all experienced moments like these, we also have the opportunity to redeem ourselves, at least partially, to set things right by making amends for our behavior by offering an apology. Offering a sincere apology can work wonders to soothe hurt feelings. However, making excuses along with an apology usually does just the opposite: it can prolong those hurt feelings and even add to them.

Here are two kinds of excuses to be on the lookout for when making an apology. The first is when you apologize and then blame the other person's behavior. It usually goes something like this: "I'm really sorry for doing that, but I wouldn't have if you didn't keep doing. . . ." While there are always two sides to every story, and while the other person may not have acted perfectly or may have also been partly at fault, blaming them for your behavior—even if justified—rarely eases anyone's feelings and definitely doesn't help to restore peace in a relationship. If you have ever done this, then you know this isn't an apology; rather, it's the start of an argument that usually turns into a long-standing one. It's always better to own up to your own actions and let the other person do the same. Remember, your behavior is the only one you can control, and at the end of the day, you want your side of the street to be clean.

The other way to ruin an apology is to give a reason—valid or not—as to why you acted a certain way or took an action. Offering excuses in this way often cancels out the apology itself and leaves the other person still feeling hurt or disappointed. We've all been on the receiving end of these kinds of excuses, and an apology backed up with a ready-made excuse is often received as a veiled threat that the offending behavior is likely to continue should the same situation occur again. Certainly, no one is satisfied, and the dispute or hurt feelings don't get resolved and often simmer, only to bubble up into a fresh disagreement later. Fortunately, there is a better way of making an apology that *does* work to set things right.

This better way is to say you're sorry without offering any kind of excuse and to show that you mean it. In other words, show your feelings of contrition with humility and honesty. When you approach people this way, they identify with you because you become vulnerable by demonstrating your awareness of your faults. Doing so makes you relatable because we all make mistakes—no one is immune. When we own our mistakes and make a sincere attempt to apologize, people generally react in kind. They usually forgive us, and that's why offering a sincere apology is so healing. It's meant to free you both from negative feelings and restore you both to peace.

The next time you find yourself acting in a way you'd rather not repeat, or when you hurt someone's feelings, intentionally or not, say you're sorry and mean it. Keep your apology squarely centered on you and your behavior, and don't ruin it by offering up an excuse or explanation. If the other person is still upset, ask what you can do to set things right, and then be willing to make a sincere attempt to follow through. While we'll all continue to act imperfectly, at least we can apologize properly and make the amends that will get us back to the harmony we all desire.

66

Choose whom you spend time with.

One of my brothers tells an interesting story of meeting a woman at a party he hosted. She came with another guest, and he didn't know her. Throughout the evening, he was struck by how calm she appeared, how self-assured and friendly she seemed. She radiated a peace he was attracted to, so later in the evening he sat down and had a chat with her, determined to find out more about her and more about the aura she projected.

She was in her early sixties and had raised her kids not far from where she was living now. When my brother commented on how centered, peaceful, and relaxed she was, she said it was the result of a decision she made several years earlier. She told him that she was reviewing her life one day, and she realized there were people in it who didn't bring her happiness: people who, in fact, brought conflict and drama, who made her feel bad about herself and were negative. She identified those who drained her energy and brought down her attitude. She said she made a decision to stop allowing these types of people to negatively affect her. From that day on, she would only spend time with people who added to her life: people who brought her happiness and made her feel good about herself and life in general. That was her secret, she told him.

My brother was struck by this simple action, and he had many questions. What about those with whom she was forced to be in a relationship, like family? She told him the key in those situations was to limit those interactions, to restrict them when possible, and to set strict boundaries where needed. She said she rarely spoke to some of her siblings these days, and she had accepted that as being for the best. The most important thing, she said, was to recognize that everyone had their own lives, and that when those lives diverge from yours, you were allowed to let them go, let them pursue what they felt was right for them. Without guilt, you set them free, and in the process, you set yourself free as well. She ended by saying that she still has a deep love for those she's let go of, and that things may change down the road. Since she's made the choice to surround herself with loving, nurturing friends and family members, however, she's enjoyed a freeness of spirit, a lightness and happiness that she treasures, and it showed.

When I heard this story, I began thinking of the various people in my life with whom I had once been close, but whose lives had diverged from mine. I realized that as we all move through life, our priorities inevitably change, and as we evolve, our opinions often change. As they do, the people we spend time with change as well. After hearing this woman's story, I began to look at those relationships that no longer added to my peace of mind or to my happiness, and I consciously began distancing myself, limiting their access to me. As I did, I attracted others into my life who appreciated whom I had become, who fed my self-esteem and contributed to the joy I look for in my life. I also realized that some people and family members had distanced themselves from me, and I accepted that. It didn't mean the love we had for one another was gone; it just meant we were on our own path. I respected that and continued down my own.

The biggest thing I took from this woman's story is that I had a choice, and I had an obligation to myself. My happiness was, and always had been, my responsibility. In exercising the power of choice over whom I spent time with, I was doing myself the greatest service I could—I was determining the course of my happiness and well-being. Ultimately, we all have this choice and responsibility to ourselves.

67

"The surest sign of wisdom is constant cheerfulness."

—Michel de Montaigne

L ife can be very serious. For years, we struggle to become independent, to establish ourselves, to raise a family, to acquire enough of a cushion to feel financially secure, and so on. As we compete in what has been called the "rat race," there's little time for levity. We are careful not to let our guard down lest someone pass us and get the recognition, the position, or all the things we're sure there aren't enough of. With social media so much a part of our lives, we're careful to post only our best photos, emphasizing the perfect life we'd like others to think we have. I once saw an influencer on YouTube who broke down and showed what actually went on behind the camera after she shot her so-called glamorous life. She pretended to be getting ready for an exciting night out on the town, and after the shoot, she took her makeup off, got into her pajamas, and crawled into bed before 8 PM. I'm reminded of a saying about the flip side of the rat race: "Even if you win the rat race, you're still a rat."

For much of my life, I was too focused on getting ahead and didn't let my guard down much. In my early career, I relentlessly pursued being the best, and being too serious for my own good, I wasn't very fun to be around most of the time. I saw all of life as one big competition for limited resources, and I had little interest in being a nice, helpful, fun-loving guy. I mean, we all know that nice guys finish last, right? As I got older, though, something interesting happened: I began to relax. I realized there actually was enough "stuff" to go around, and I found that the more I let go, and the more I helped other people, the more successful I became and the more I enjoyed myself. The biggest example of this was meeting my wife later in life. My sister, who mostly knew my serious side, warned me to "not be so serious" around her. My wife and I laugh at that now because she thinks I'm the funniest guy she's ever met!

What happened for me is what we see in a lot of older people: the things we once thought were so important just aren't. Instead, the things we took for granted for years—good health, lazy dinners with friends, the promise of a Saturday morning—were always the most precious things in life, and now that we're older, we enjoy and appreciate them more. Many of us know an older uncle or grandparent or elderly neighbor who radiates a calm, a cheerfulness that reveals the wisdom that comes with age and experience. The good news is that you don't have to wait for years to release the joy that's inside of you. At any moment in your day, you can stop and let your guard down and relax a bit. Go ahead and join in the laughter around you, or better yet, learn to laugh more at yourself. Being more cheerful surely is a sign of being wiser, and it's something you can begin cultivating right now.

68

Seek ways to be of service.

One concept that always changes my interactions with people is when I shift from an attitude of "What's in it for me?" to "How can I be of service?" When I started my business several years ago, it was sometimes a grind to have to prospect to find new clients. Many mornings, I'd wake up dreading a day of cold-calling companies, trying to uncover a need or a fit for what I was selling at the time. One day, though, I reframed my attitude from trying to sell things to looking for companies or people I could be of service to and help. While my pitch remained essentially the same, this change of focus and intent had a dramatic and immediate effect. Suddenly, I didn't take the rejection I always got so personally; instead, I just told myself they didn't need my help that day. Then when I did find someone with a need and interest, I was able to put on a helping hat rather than a selling hat. This made the interaction more authentic and resulted in a much better experience for us both.

Looking for ways to be of service in other areas of life pays off as well. Whenever I go to a party these days, I make a beeline to the kitchen and begin helping the host with their preparations. There are always things to do, like setting things out on tables, helping to prepare appetizers, or assisting with the drinks, and so on. While the host usually says they don't need help, I find there are still many things I can do to make things easier on them. In addition to feeling useful and a part of the gathering, being helpful in this way gives me a chance to interact with all the guests, and this is especially useful when I don't know a lot of people. Also, there are plenty of opportunities to help throughout the party like clearing plates, setting other food items out, or assisting older people with seconds or by refreshing their drinks, and so forth. I always find I've enjoyed a party much more when I participate in this way.

At home, there are endless opportunities to be of service—even if it's not my chore or my day to do something. I don't mean you should do others' chores for them; however, if you have an opportunity to lighten someone else's burden one day, go ahead and do it. They will greatly appreciate the little gesture you've made, and you may even find they return the favor. Doing little things like this around the house is the easiest way to reduce tension and create a more harmonious home.

Looking for ways to be of service is so gratifying that I now make it my focus whenever I'm out in public. When I arrive at a doctor's office, I always hold the door open for people behind me, and then step aside and let them go in first. It's an unexpected gesture, and it's enjoyable watching the surprise and smiles on their faces. Checking in and interacting with the receptionists presents another opportunity to be of service in a more subtle way. I'm quick to compliment someone who has obviously spent time and money on their appearance, or who has a good attitude. If they seem to be in a bad mood, I attempt to empathize with them. My attitude is that if I were working at that same counter eight hours a day, I'd want someone to be nice to me!

There's an old saying that what goes around comes around, and I believe that's true. The more we can extend ourselves by helping others, the more we help ourselves by receiving grateful looks and smiles and thereby creating a kinder world. Just imagine if everyone sought ways of being of service and helping others. That's the world I want to live in, and since I'm part of this world, let it begin with me.

You don't know
what you don't know.

I have a very good friend who for years used to tell me this. We'd be out to dinner together, sometimes with a group of friends, and I'd discuss a challenging situation I was going through or contemplating changes I needed to make. She'd always say, "Well, you should remain open. You don't know what you don't know." At the time, this didn't resonate with me, and I didn't really understand what she meant. What I failed to realize is that she was talking about resistance to change.

Change can be a scary thing. You never know if doing things differently or getting something else will be better or worse than what you may be doing or what you have now. We all have examples of making a change that didn't work out: we've changed jobs and then longed for our old one. We've moved, changed partners, cars, and more. While some of these changes worked out, what's interesting is that we tend to remember the changes that didn't work out more often. As we get older, it's these changes that weigh more heavily on us and influence our future decisions.

When we were younger, change was not only easier, it was an expected part of the process for growing and developing. We were anxious, willing, and enthusiastic to try new things. We didn't have a lot of experience weighing us down, and we had a lot of time to recover from any bad decisions we made. But the older and wiser we get, the more resistant we become to making changes. That's where my friend's suggestion comes in. By constantly reminding myself that I don't know what I don't know, I keep open the door to change, to trying something new. While I may think I know how something may go, and while I may even have experience that points to a particular outcome, it's equally true that I simply don't know for sure until I try it.

What's more, another friend gave me some great advice that also helps me when I'm not sure if I should try something new. She says she has a simple test she uses whenever she's hesitant to make a change. She asks herself if the change is reversible or not. She says many decisions can be reversed if they don't go the way she anticipated they would. If she decides to buy a new car, for example, and she doesn't like it, then she can sell it and buy the previous model again. Same with cutting her hair short—if she doesn't like it, it will grow back. But, if she decided to have a tooth removed instead of, say, having a root canal, then that is an irreversible decision. She says any irreversible decision requires a lot more thought, but decisions that can be reversed, she's much more open to making. Obviously, there are degrees to this simple paradigm. Selling a house in a nice neighborhood may be somewhat reversible: you might be able to buy back into the neighborhood, just not the exact house—at least right away. Overall, though, I've found this general concept helpful in deciding whether to change something or not.

What I've also found helpful is remembering that I truly don't know what I don't know. Regardless of my past experiences and all the education and knowledge I've accumulated, there are still a lot of variables I can't account for, a lot of things that can go either way, and it's important to remember that I'm also constantly changing as well. When I remember that I can't know for sure how something will go until I try it, then I'm often more willing to remain open and take a chance. By remaining open, I've been able to retain some of the wonder and spontaneity of my youth, and it's led to some truly wonderful experiences in my life—like overcoming my resistance to online dating that led to finding my wonderful wife.

The next time you're faced with a change or a decision, before you say no, remind yourself that you don't know what you don't know. You might be more willing to try it—and that could turn out to be a wonderful thing for you.

70

Share a memory with someone you love.

Too often, too much time goes by before we sincerely pay someone we love a compliment, tell them how much they mean to us, or how much we love them. One of the reasons I hear for this is that people don't know how to stop and share their feelings honestly without becoming embarrassed or without making the other person feel obligated to respond in kind. "They know I love them," they say, "I tell them all the time." Saying the obligatory "I love you" can lose its impact over the years, and when we hear it ourselves, it often doesn't register. There is, however, one easy way to connect with someone, and that is by sharing a special memory you have together.

An example is a memory my sister and I share. While we live on opposite sides of the country now, we still text and speak a few times a month, and we generally know what's happening in each other's lives. But what gets lost in these surface communications is the depth of our shared history and experience. All of that can quickly be revived, though, by sharing one simple story. When I was much younger, right after my sister moved into her own apartment, she invited me over for dinner. Her signature meal was a tuna casserole, and she had spent the afternoon preparing it. Her apartment smelled wonderful when I got there, and several hours later we sat down to eat. After a few bites, my sister looked up and said, "I don't know, it just doesn't taste the same." I had the same thought, and after she poked around at the casserole, she raised her eyebrows, started laughing, and said, "I forgot the tuna!" We both had a long belly laugh over that one, and the giggles bubbled up throughout the evening. Even now, years later, relating that story brings back not only the hilarity of that moment but also the closeness we shared during those years. It was a unique snippet in time, and in a way, it defined our youth, our love, and our history together.

Memories like this—and hundreds of others—have an incredible power to unite us, to inspire us, and to help us share deep feelings of love and belonging. We all have them, and not just with family members. When I want to connect with a dear friend I haven't spoken to in a while, I can call and leave a message letting her know I was thinking about the wonderful times we'd hiked Mt. Rainier together and that I miss her. Or I can leave a quick message for another friend about the time his old, white VW Scirocco almost died in the line at the Mexican border crossing and how worried we both were but how much we laughed about it later. When you begin thinking about these memories, you'll find you have many opportunities to connect with those you love and how much people will gain by hearing from you.

Today, think of someone who hasn't heard from you in a while, think of a cherished memory, and then call or visit them or send them an email or text, and share that memory. Your friend or loved one will be pleasantly surprised, and you'll be able to share your love and appreciation for them in a warm and memorable way. It'll make their day—and yours, too.

71

"Think in the morning.
Act in the noon. Eat in the
evening. Sleep in the night."

—William Blake

I breathed a deep sigh of relief the first time I read this quote. At the time, I had been struggling with a complicated life, multi-tasking family, business, creativity, spirituality, all jumbled and mixed in every hour of each day. Between the immediacy and volume of business communications and emails, personal texting and social media postings, I found it hard to compartmentalize things, and subjects that were on my mind when I woke up, like work, were still there when I laid my head on my pillow. Trying to juggle everything and still find time for some peaceful contemplation, for some renewal of spirit, seemed impossible most days. I paid the price for this by feeling a persistent uneasiness, a sense that things might never settle down, and that I may lose my chance at happiness. That's when I read this quote.

How simple Blake made it all seem! As I spent some time with this, I saw that my days could indeed be broken up into these broad categories. While everyone is different, of course, what I found is that I am the most creative in the morning. I'm writing this now on a Thursday morning, and this is the time when my ideas flow. Previously, I had tried to write later in the day, once the workday finished, but I struggled with that. Thinking and creating in the morning just fits my natural rhythm, and today I've learned to honor that, even if it means getting up earlier to make time for it. By doing this, I achieve a deep sense of accomplishment that sets me up to act in the noon. For me, this means being active in all areas of my life: business, physically, dealing with family, etc. My "noon" can start as early as 9 AM on through the end of the working day, and if I've thought enough in the morning, my mind is much clearer, more focused, and easily trained on the tasks that require action. Besides having the most energy during the day, I also find other people are focused on activity during that time as well, and it's easy to feed off one another.

"Eat in the evening" instantly reminded me of the seemingly lost practice of eating dinner together as a family, or even at the same time as my spouse. Before making this a priority, business obligations or trying to fit the gym in often bled over into dinnertime. As mentioned earlier, trying to think or be creative at this time didn't work for me either; instead, it isolated me, often frustrating me by my lack of creative work. Changing the time I did this, however, immediately freed me up to be present with those I loved, and by spending dedicated time with them each evening, I received the emotional nourishment I had been lacking and that I needed.

Perhaps the most impactful part of Blake's saying is the "sleep in the night" part. It can be hard to shut the mind off, as we know. If I remind myself that it's now the night, and my only job is to sleep, I'm able to give myself permission to do what comes naturally anyway: sleep in the night. Simple, yet amazingly effective. We all have complicated lives, and multitasking seems to be the only way to get things done these days. By breaking our days down to match our natural rhythms, you'll find that life gets easier, more manageable. Examine your own rhythms, and see where you can simplify your life as well. You'll find more room for the peace and calm you've been looking for.

It is what it is, but it will become what you make it.

We all have our crosses to bear. Some of us have had difficult childhoods, and we're still trying to make peace with those; for others, relationships have been challenging. There are divorces, children with hurt feelings, and many other complicated situations. Many of us have or are struggling with finding the right direction in our lives—which career to pick, or whether to leave unfulfilling ones. Sometimes, when faced with looking at things as they are, it's difficult to see beyond that. It's tempting to just say, "Well, it is what it is," and then resign ourselves to these unsatisfying circumstances. There is another way, though.

The world is full of stories of people who rose up through difficult beginnings, or who were able to remake themselves after many failed attempts. One of my favorites is a guy named Ray Kroc. At fifty-two years old, Ray's life looked as if it was over. He was a failed paper cup salesman, a real estate broker, a piano player, and a milkshake mixer salesman. Physically, he seemed at a bottom as well: he had diabetes and incipient arthritis; his gallbladder was removed as well as most of his thyroid gland. I'm not sure what many of us would have done given his situation; however, Ray had the unshakable belief that the best was still ahead of him. As some of you know, Ray turned out quite well. He went on to build a chain of successful fast-food restaurants that we're all familiar with today: McDonald's.

At forty-two years old, I, too, was at a bottom in my life. Unemployed, unmarried, broke, and without direction, life seemed pretty bleak. Hearing today's quote at that time reminded me that my past didn't have to become my future, and that by taking steps in the right direction, I could change what my future would look like and what I could become. I was taught to be patient. My therapist at the time told me that it took forty years to get to this point, and that it might take a few years to change it. If I worked steadily toward goals that I felt were right for me, though, then my future could become anything I choose to make it.

Fast forward just ten years, and my life completely transformed. I found and married the love of my life, started my own business on my terms, and even discovered and pursued a love of writing. If you are struggling with things the way they are, don't lose hope and don't give in to the thinking that they'll always be this way. Instead, get the support you need (career coach, therapist, personal trainer, etc.), have faith, and take consistent action toward what has meaning for you. Remember, the world is full of new beginnings and happy endings, and your life can still become what you want to make it.

73

The difference between heaven and hell.

The concept of heaven and hell has been around for more than two millennia, as have the various interpretations of them. Some believe heaven and hell are physical destinations we are sent to when we die; others believe heaven and hell are states of consciousness we enter in and out of right here on earth. Certainly, we have all experienced highs and lows, those times when we've felt the grace of heaven shine in our lives, and those other times when unspeakable tragedy has touched us or someone close to us. Years ago, I heard a story of the difference between heaven and hell that always stuck with me, because it taught me a truth that resonates with me to this day. It goes like this:

A man was once given a tour of both heaven and hell. The tour started in hell, which was laid out with endless banquet tables featuring the most varied and delicious foods you could imagine. There were perfectly prepared meats of all varieties, along with delicious vegetables prepared with any sauce you wanted. There were rooms filled with cuisines from around the world: Italian, French, Asian, Mexican . . . anything you desired. You could eat as much as you wanted, and you never got full or sick or fat—just an endless experience of dining on the most satisfying and delicious foods imaginable. The aromas made your mouth water. There was just one problem though: each person's arms had been replaced with a four-foot-long fork and spoon, and they were too long to feed themselves. Everyone in hell, therefore, starved each day while surrounded by this infinite array of exquisite food.

The next stop on the tour was heaven. At first, heaven looked a lot like hell: endless banquet rooms filled with tables of delicious, perfectly prepared foods. One whole room had an endless display of Thanksgiving foods—turkey, gravies of all kinds, mashed potatoes, candied yams, green beans with a savory dried onion topping, and a whole other room had desserts, including pecan pies, apple pies, cherry pies, and every ice cream flavor imaginable. Here, too, you could gorge yourself without getting full, sick, or fat—nothing except endless pleasure. As in hell, each person's arms had been replaced with four-foot-long forks and spoons, but in heaven, no one starved. The reason for this is that no one in heaven thought of feeding themselves; instead, they each cooperated and fed one another. In this way, they all enjoyed the exquisite food, were nourished both physically and emotionally, and thus they lived in bliss.

When I heard this story the first time, it made perfect sense, though I was surprised I didn't see the solution coming. Of course! This is exactly my experience as well. The more I seek to help another, the closer I get to the peace and serenity I've always thought heaven held. The more I withdraw and try to feed myself only, the more miserable I become. If you ever find yourself in a low mood or feeling ungrateful for what you have or don't have, think back to this story and ask yourself who you can feed today. Then, reach out to that person and offer emotional, physical, or spiritual food to them. The moment you do, you will both be lifted to heaven, right here on Earth.

74

Become willing.

I t's easy to get locked into a position or an opinion and then refuse
to consider other possibilities. This is especially true if we have
tried something and failed at it in the past, or if we decided we
didn't like something, like the taste of Thousand Island dressing. But
isn't it also true that things you wouldn't eat when you were younger
you now enjoy today? I'll bet you've also found that there were activities you didn't think you would enjoy, yet when you were encouraged
to try them, you found you kind of liked them, too. This happens to
all of us, and the underlying concept is that we constantly grow and
change, and what must also change is our willingness to be open to
new things. Someone once said we aren't human *beings*, we're really
human *becomings*.

A suggestion I give people who seem stuck or unhappy in their
lives is to become willing to consider doing things they normally
would reject outright. I'm not saying they should say yes to everything; rather, don't say an automatic no, and instead move to a maybe.
In other words, become willing to at least consider doing something
you may not think you'd enjoy or might never see yourself doing.

A prime example of this happened years ago when I was single.
A very good friend and close adviser of mine recommended I try online dating. "No way!" was my response. I'd tried it before and found
it to not only be ineffective but also a little humiliating as well. There
was just no way I'd consider it again. My friend was patient with me

and asked if I could at least be willing to give it a try. I said I'd think about it. I resisted for weeks until one morning I was out to break-fast with a group of people, and a woman shared about a new online dating site she was on. She said she hadn't met anyone yet she'd want to date long term; however, the quality of people she did meet was quite high. Overall, it had been a pleasant experience for her. At that moment, my willingness to at least be open to the idea kicked in, and I asked her what site it was. I spoke with my friend about it again, and I decided I'd give it a go. Literally two weeks after posting my profile on the site, I was on a date and sitting across the table from my future wife. We've now spent over a decade together, and neither of us have ever been happier! And I owe it all to being willing to try something that I thought for sure wasn't for me.

Willingness is a skill that sometimes takes a little work and prac-tice to become comfortable with. I've found that what helps if I'm simply not ready or willing yet is to try to get to a place where I can become willing to *be* willing. My experience is that if I can just keep the door to possibility open even a crack, then curiosity often opens it a bit more later on. Being willing to be willing is still much better than no, and I've used this technique over and over again to give my-self a chance to explore new things.

Willingness can help us in all areas of our lives, too: being will-ing to consider someone else's point of view, connect with someone, give them a ride, or extend ourselves in some way. Even something small like trying an ethnic restaurant we've never been in before can bring wonderful surprises. Life truly is a smorgasbord, and while I don't recommend you eat everything, I do recommend you become willing to try more things. It's a way to enjoy the banquet of life and a way to stay younger in spirit. And it all starts by simply becoming more willing.

75

Feed your mind as carefully as you feed your stomach.

How would you feel if you tripled your caffeine intake in the morning and skipped breakfast? What would your mood and energy level be like around 10:00 AM? Now, think about how you'd feel if at lunchtime you went to the greasiest food chain you can think of and had a chili cheeseburger and chili fries. How are you feeling around 2:30 PM as that settles in your stomach? Imagine yourself stopping by the local coffee shop on the way home and ordering a large coffee and adding a shot of espresso, and then either skipping dinner completely or pigging out on a pint of ice cream. How are you around your family tonight? Comfortable and easygoing, or agitated and short-tempered? It's easy to play this scenario out and to imagine how we'd be if we then repeated this the next day or skipped eating that day altogether. At some point, we wouldn't be able to function at all. While this is clear to most of us, what we tend to forget is that the mind needs proper nourishment just as much as our bodies do.

While we constantly feed the mind with our random thoughts, what we often neglect to do is purposefully feed it the right kind of diet. Instead, we tend to binge watch and follow the news or current events, all of which feature the worst of what we're capable of, and that reinforces a sense of hopelessness and gets us asking, "What's the point?" We also tend to feed our minds self-defeating thoughts made up of worries and fears, or we spend time reviewing the past, regretting or wishing things had turned out differently. After a steady diet of negativity, we begin acting on the pictures we've been painting, and it becomes easy for us to treat others poorly, to lose our temper, or even become depressed. And it all has to do with the kind of mental diet we're consuming.

Like our bodies, our minds instantly respond to the quality of food we feed it. The moment you stop eating junk food and instead eat a nourishing, healthy meal, you immediately feel better. It's the same with your mind. The moment you go on a healthy, nourishing mental diet, you instantly gain a better outlook, your attitude improves, and suddenly the future isn't as dark as it was just hours or days ago. Many of us underestimate the power our mental diet has. We get in the habit of bingeing on mental junk food, and we suffer the consequences.

Luckily, there is an immediate and proven solution: commit to and begin a better mental diet today. A couple of ways to start include looking at all the negative things you're taking in now and stop indulging in them. If you're a big consumer of the news, give yourself a thirty-day cease-and-desist from viewing or reading it. This will have an immediate positive impact on your attitude. Next, purposefully choose and begin reading, listening to podcasts, or watching videos of positive stories or spiritually nourishing material. The world is full of uplifting, affirming messages, and by searching these out and consuming them daily, they will reinforce and build your awareness of all the good in the world—and inside yourself. Nature is also a wonderful place to look for the good. If humanity is bringing you down, simply step outside, find a friendly spider or caterpillar or bumble-bee, and watch them innocently and diligently work away, oblivious to everything else. Each is a miracle and never fails to restore my perspective whenever I take the time to be with them.

Remember: what you feed your mental and spiritual self, and how often you do, greatly affects your moods and your life experience. If you're not feeling grateful, hopeful, or helpful, consider changing your mental diet for the next thirty days. You'll notice a change for the good almost immediately.

76

Life is tough because you get the test first and then the lesson.

In school, we spend a lot of time reading textbooks, attending lectures, taking notes, and going to study sessions, all in preparation to take tests to determine what we learned. In college, I used to love the official notetakers whose job it was to take and then distribute lecture notes, which I would compare with the notes I'd taken. When I had questions or didn't understand a concept in the reading (and this was especially true in advanced mathematics), I could visit the professors at office hours to receive help to find the answers. Long before midterms or final exams, I'd spend days studying so I could do well on the upcoming tests. When that day arrived, I felt prepared and confident that I had done all I could to be ready to succeed. If only life worked this way.

When we leave the school environment, we find that life works the opposite way. Each day is different and gives us new situations we've not had time to study and prepare for. Out of the blue will come a test of some kind: a work situation or problem to solve; a challenge in an intimate relationship will surface; a problem with your house or car will suddenly appear, etc., and you will be forced to address it—without the benefit of careful preparation, study, or advanced notice.

While these situations can be vexing, what's even more challenging is that after each of these tests, a lesson follows. Perhaps we should have paid more attention to how the software at our job works, or been more aware of how our actions might affect others close to us, or actually had our car serviced when the manual suggested. The difficult thing about the lesson following the test is that if we don't learn it, the test will be repeated. Sooner or later, we'll find that we're running into the same issue in our relationships, this time perhaps with a coworker or neighbor or friend. While the tests in life will always come before the lessons, and they'll repeat until we learn their lessons, thankfully after each one, we have the opportunity to step back and learn from them.

These days, I allow myself the room to look at the tests I've failed or that I didn't handle the way I'd like to have. I carefully think about what occurred, look for where I was wrong in a situation, and ask myself what I need to change for next time. And that time surely comes. In the end, life will always give us new tests, and that's how we grow and learn. When each test comes, we should ask ourselves: What's the lesson? What is life trying to teach me right now? As soon as we can answer that, we can study for the next one and be on the lookout for a different form it might take. If we're prepared, we might just pass that test because we've learned the lesson it was trying to teach us last time.

77

Easy does it.

Some of you may have seen this bumper sticker on a car in front of you when driving around town or stopped at a light. Whenever I do, it immediately reminds me to slow down, to become more present. It also draws my attention to what my emotional state was like before seeing it. Like most people, I'm usually in a hurry, rushing from one place to the next, often lost in thought as I multitask the next ten things I'm going to do. Others relate a similar pattern of thinking, planning, or hurrying from one appointment to the next. The idea of taking it easy is the last thing on their minds. Because of how we're all wired today—quick texts, fifteen-second ads, and more—the idea of slowing down and taking it easy seems counterproductive to effectively doing anything. And that's a shame.

Society continually works against the idea of slowing down and taking it easy. Markets, convenience stores, and even gas stations now have videos to distract you from what you're doing, all anxious to capture your limited attention, to sell you something or remind you of what you could or should be doing instead, such as taking that cruise to Alaska or that river trip in Europe. This constant conditioning to be busy nudges us when we finally do have some downtime, and we're quick to grab our phones and chase the latest news stories. The rush to keep current on everything, to not be left out, never seems to leave us. Truly taking it easy, just being present, seems to be something we've forgotten how to do, and with that forgetting, we've lost the capacity to be at peace, to be content. But we can retrain ourselves to do just that, and today's simple saying holds the key.

"Easy does it" is a phrase that describes an action, so it doesn't mean you need to stop doing everything and start meditating all day. Far from it. Instead, it suggests that we can still do all the things we need to, just with less stress and pressure. In other words, we don't need to treat everything as if we're racing against a stopwatch. We don't have to text someone right back, and we don't have to like every post or hurry through the line at the grocery store. We can take our time with our regular activities; give them the care and attention they deserve. By retraining yourself to be present and gently aware of what you're doing right now, you discover the spiritual tool of mindfulness. Mindfulness allows you to access peace and contentment this very moment, regardless of what you're doing.

By practicing this simple strategy, you will also add joy and meaning into all of your activities. Doing things purposefully gives you back the time and space the world tries to steal from you, and regaining these precious moments of your life adds a depth to them you'll come to appreciate and welcome. As you go through your day today, consciously remind yourself to take it easy, slow down, and become aware of the minutes that used to rush by unnoticed. As you create this space, calm will return, and you'll remember that each moment is precious and holds meaning. So go out and live this day, and remember, "Easy does it." Life is better that way.

If at first you don't succeed, you're perfectly normal.

F ear of failure keeps a lot of us from trying new things and, as a result, keeps many of us stuck in life. While we may not love our current job, at least it pays the bills; besides, what if we can't find a better one? Should we pursue a degree or follow an idea we've had for years? Too much risk—it's safer to stay where we are. Sometimes it seems easier to live with the hope, the dream, and even the fear than to try something new.

The trick to moving past the fear of failure is to reframe it. A great example of this is what Thomas Edison once said when asked about all the failures he had endured on his way to discovering the lightbulb. He was renowned for conducting over 10,000 "failed experiments." He said, "I have not failed. I've just found 10,000 ways that won't work." When viewed this way, we see that trying and "failing" is critical to accomplishing anything. Kids are a great example of this. They stumble and fall hundreds of times before learning to walk and run. Think of your own experience of learning to ride a bicycle—did you ever wobble and fall? We all did, and this was part of the process of learning. Somehow, we've forgotten this as we've grown older. That's where reframing comes in handy.

The key to making changes in our lives, to trying new things and enjoying our lives more fully, is remembering that failing first is the way we succeed later. Sure, you may discover what won't work, but it's the only way to find out what will. Reframing failure in this way normalizes our experiences and frees us from the fear of embarrassment or temporary setbacks. It also helps us embrace the experience of learning and growing. Try keeping this in mind the next time you enter a new situation or challenge. Remember, if at first you don't succeed, you're perfectly normal.

79

Rediscover the joy of reading.

When was the last time you sat down to read something? I mean, something other than a social media post or the news feed headlines on your cell phone. Reading, and the deep enjoyment and enrichment it brings, is an increasingly rare pastime these days. It's easy to fall out of the habit of setting aside the time to read or even identifying a particular book or genre of books you're interested in exploring. For years, I fell out of it, too. I forgot how much I missed—and needed—reading until I was in the middle of a nightmare home renovation, and I was complaining to my older brother one night. He asked me an odd question, "What book are you reading?" I didn't understand the question at first, so he explained that it would help to open another window in my reality and that an escape into a new world—a world any good book would offer me—was just what I needed. I took his advice and found that book, and so instead of complaining about the remodel each night, I spent my evenings chasing a serial killer through Chicago in the late nineteenth century by reading *The Devil in the White City*. That's when I rediscovered the joy and purpose of reading.

Reading is, for many, one of our first coping skills. We often discover the joy of reading as children, and we use it to be entertained, to escape, and to learn more about how other people deal with the same kinds of situations or emotions we face. As we share a character's journey, we gain access to new ways of thinking and to solutions we wouldn't have thought about on our own. Reading is like living a whole other life in a different land or time, and we gain new skills, ideas, and experience by reading about someone else's reality. I'm sure you still remember the impact, the feelings, and the joy good books have brought you over the years.

In addition to the immersive escape and introduction to new life skills reading provides, it also gives us a valuable new perspective on not only life in general but, more importantly, on our own personal experience. The comedian Bill Maher once said, "If you think you have it tough, read history books." Whenever I do, I'm appalled at what the mass of humanity has had to deal with and overcome in their lives. Just the fact that anesthesia wasn't available until the latter part of the nineteenth century is a horrifying thought. For most, a tooth extraction was not only a terrifying event but a potentially deadly one as well. Just think, surgeries of all kinds, including amputations, were performed with the patient wide-awake! By providing this kind of perspective, reading has the unique ability to instantly add gratitude into your life. Suddenly, what you have to go through seems infinitely easier than what others have struggled with, and if they could survive and succeed, so can you.

Renewing the habit of reading can be done in a variety of ways. I started by reading a half hour each night before bed. The house was quiet, no one needed my attention, and it was easy to put my phone down and pick up a book instead. Some people who have time in the morning prefer to read then, while they're fresh and before they get too sidetracked. If you're looking for time in your day to read, you can easily find some by observing your video or cell phone usage, and switch some of that time to reading. Even a half hour is a good start.

If you commute, audio books are a great choice. You'll find you can get through several books a year that way alone.

Regardless of how you bring the joy of reading back into your life, you will be enriched in countless ways once you start. You might consider that your local library may have monthly book selections, along with book discussion groups. Here you'll not only find interesting books to read but also a new community of potential friends with similar interests. In addition, you probably even have books at home you bought with the intention of enjoying at some point. Those books are still calling to you, and once you dive in, they will reveal their treasures. What are you waiting for?

80

You become what you dwell on most.

There is a school of thought that has been around for many years called the Law of Attraction. Essentially, it states that we are all co-creators of our lives and circumstances, and that we draw to us those things we think about most. Moreover, we attract these things in direct proportion to the level of feelings and belief we have in them. There are hundreds of books, podcasts, and videos that explain this theory in detail, and a couple of my favorites include one of the originals, *As a Man Thinketh*, by James Allen, and a more recent book, *The Secret*, by Rhonda Byrne. If you haven't read any of these titles, I recommend you look into them. One complaint about this concept is that it's too mysterious, some even call it New Age; however, as you learn a little more about it, and then begin practicing some of its principles, my experience is that you'll get some immediate and remarkable results.

To start with, I've learned that the whole idea of attracting something into your life isn't mysterious at all; in fact, it's based on a scientific finding called the reticular activating system—RAS for short. The RAS is a web-shaped group of cells, the size of a walnut, located in the base of the brain. Its function is to help you focus by filtering out the thousands of sensory perceptions bombarding us at any second. The only data that get through are what you've identified is important to you—in a sense, you will attract the information that has the most meaning to you. To demonstrate this, perform this quick experiment in real time (or with someone else). Turn your cell phone over now and write down everything you can remember that's on the home page—background, colors, apps, etc. Once you do that, pick up your phone and see how many you remembered. Then, quickly, turn it back over again. (If you're doing this experiment now, don't read the next sentence until you do.) Now, with your phone turned over, write down the exact time. I'll bet most of you didn't notice the time when you checked your home page, did you? That's because you weren't *looking* for that information, so it didn't get through your RAS.

The point here is that all the resources you need to accomplish any goal are out there and available to you at all times. If you're not focusing or dwelling on them, they won't get through your RAS, and you won't attract them. The other component of the Law of Attraction is that the more feeling and belief you attach to a goal, the faster you will manifest it. You paint your goals and dreams with feelings by the self-talk you use when thinking about them. The words you say to yourself have immense power. That saying you learned in school, "Sticks and stones will break my bones, but words will never hurt me" is untrue. Bones heal, yet we all remember things said to us years ago, and we can relive and feel their impact even today. When we combine a goal with a belief and then dwell on the accomplishment of that goal with deep feelings, we begin to attract that into our lives.

Whether you know it or not, you're using the Law of Attraction even now. Isn't it true that everything you're thinking about most is happening in your life right now? Some of you may say, "Yes, but I'm thinking about it because it's already *in* my life." What if it was the other way around, though? What if you could change your life by changing your thinking? The idea that you can change your life circumstances, and so your destiny, by altering what you dwell on and believe is perhaps the greatest discovery of humankind. I encourage you to learn more about it (or reengage with this great truth) and begin consciously dwelling on how you'd like your life to be—pursuing your most meaningful goals, practicing a healthier lifestyle, attracting more peace and harmony into your life—whatever speaks to *you*. Combined with taking consistent action, this is a sure way to make your dreams come true.

81

"Don't let yesterday use up too much of today."

—Will Rogers

My oldest brother once told me of his tendency to some-times wake up in the morning and, while still lying in bed, mentally "touch all the old bruises." He'd review the missed opportunities from previous weeks, months, or years; then he'd review the wrongs he suffered—both real and imagined—in the past; then he'd go over everything in his life that wasn't the way he wanted it. He said that by the time he got out of bed, he was already exhausted!

Caroline Myss, a wonderful spiritual writer and teacher, talks about waking up with a set amount of spiritual energy each day. To simplify it here, let's just say every morning you start with 100 units of energy to use during the day. As you lie in bed reviewing the past, you use some of that spiritual energy, and as you go through your day dwelling on or reviewing or regretting the past, you further deplete that set amount of energy. This is one of the reasons we can become overwhelmed so easily on some days—our spiritual well isn't suffi-ciently full enough for us to handle the current emotional demands and tasks of the day. Allowing yesterday to use up too much of today also deprives us of the ability to be present, take in, and appreciate the people, opportunities, and gifts that are available to us each day.

Finding that balance of looking at our pasts and leveraging the lessons and experience it offers us can be difficult. I continually use the saying we mentioned earlier: "It's okay to look at the past; just don't stare." Think about how much energy you use reviewing your past, and then ask yourself what lessons you're going to take from it to live more purposefully today. Consider the 100 units of spiritual energy you get each day and dedicate no more than perhaps 10 or 15 percent of your time and energy to looking at the past. To determine how much of my 100 units I'm using on the past, for example, I simply look at how often during the hour or day I find myself returning there. If I find myself there multiple times a day, I consciously become present to what is happening right now, and I stay there so yesterday doesn't use up too much of today.

82

It all works out in the end.
If it hasn't worked out yet,
it's not the end.

There's a saying in life that "time heals all," and while I have found this to be generally true, when we're going through something difficult, it's easy to lose this perspective. Small problems or inconveniences or even temporary setbacks can sometimes seem insurmountable, and many of us have a tendency to blow them out of proportion. If something carries on for a few days or weeks or, heaven forbid, a few months, it can be easy to think the issue is never going to be resolved. As soon as we bring in the perspective of time, however, isn't it interesting how things we thought were never going to get settled, were never going to work out, have indeed been resolved? Just think back—can you remember what you were worried about a year or two ago? I'll bet most, if not all, of your so-called problems worked out sooner than you thought they would.

In order to prove this to myself, I started a habit years ago, during my journaling in the morning. What I do is make a list of the things I'm currently worrying about—issues, problems, setbacks that aren't resolved yet. I make two columns: the first is to list the actual problem or concern, and the second I leave blank so I can record the date and what happened with the issue or problem later. What's so empowering about this is that very few items remain unresolved for more than a month or two. Often, in fact, over the course of a week, more than half the items are no longer problems at all. Having them in a journal allows me to review the evidence, as it were, and to verify that time is indeed the great healer. I've found that if something hasn't worked out yet, all I have to do is give it more time.

Even the bigger issues in life: unresolved relationships, health issues, major career challenges, and so on, also tend to work out, although they can take a little more time to do so. In addition to taking more time, what's important to remember is that sometimes the way these things work out might not be the exact way we hoped for or imagined they would. There have been some close personal relationships in my life that drifted apart, and I waited years for them to mend. What I found is that, in the end, while these relationships may not have been resolved in the way I thought they would, something else happened: they changed in unexpected ways. Some toned down, and contact became less frequent, less intimate, yet we still had the core connection we had built up over the years. Other relationships became more distant as both of us had changed and moved in different ways. In each instance, however, and with the perspective of time, I saw that each of these relationships had worked out the way they should—for now.

That part, "for now," is important to remember because with any unresolved issues in our lives, it's usually not the end yet. So much in life is fluid, people and situations constantly change, and with changes come solutions and resolutions we often can't predict. When I go back to my many lists of so-called problems, I can tell you that more than 98 percent of them worked out in the end, and the other 2 percent are in the process of working out right now. What I need to do is maintain the perspective of time and think back to my actual experience of how things tend to resolve themselves, and then remind myself that if I'm still worrying about something not working out, then it's probably not the end yet.

But that day is coming.

83

Cultivate daily self-care.

Years ago, a business coach, Michael Neill, introduced me to the concept of incorporating daily self-care into my schedule. At first, I was surprised by his suggestion. Self-care in business planning? I thought we were going to concentrate on strategic goals and developing weekly processes and priorities for scaling my business. We did all that, of course, and in developing a list of priorities to achieve those goals, he suggested that a focus on daily self-care should be my number-one priority.

At first, I resisted this idea and had all the reasons why it was impractical. There already weren't enough hours in the day to get everything done on my to-do list, so how could I possibly fit in a regimen of daily self-care? Besides, what the heck was self-care anyway? What role could it possibly have in helping me grow a successful business? My coach explained that if I was going to be efficient at accomplishing all those to-dos, and if I wanted to remain sane and healthy doing so, then taking care of myself needed to become something I focused on each and every day. He said he knew of many business owners who had been able to bully their way to success, but they paid a terrible price as they neglected their homes, their relationships, their health, and other crucial elements of a life worth having. Balance, he said, was the key to overall success.

I started by making a list of ten things I could do for myself each day. The self-care items were meant to help nourish me in an

227

emotional, physical, creative, or spiritual way. He suggested that the majority of the items should be things I could do in any given day; however, one or two things—bigger things that might take more time or planning—could be a goal for the week. I started by identifying small items that would have a big impact on my day-to-day functioning. This list included getting seven to eight hours of sleep each night; eating a healthy breakfast; limiting my coffee intake to two cups of coffee each day; no caffeine after 11 AM; and getting out of the office for a half hour each day. I decided that eating outside or taking a walk after lunch or anytime I felt the need to reduce stress would be helpful. This list went on to include meditating at night, spending an hour or two of quality time with my wife, etc. The larger things included getting a massage once a week or going to the gym three or four days a week. My task was simple: I was to keep track of how many of these items I accomplished each day.

At first, I was surprised by how hard it was to remember to take care of myself. Once I got wrapped up in the activities of the day, I often forgot to even look at my list. As the days and weeks went by, however, I began remembering to do things for myself, and the results were immediate and gratifying. For instance, one self-care habit I began was taking a half-hour walk after lunch. I never used to leave my desk (let alone the office!) during the day. Getting out into the sunshine, or even the rain, had a big effect on both my problem-solving skills and my attitude. Having the time to think through issues, without someone interrupting or needing my time or attention, was liberating, and I came up with some great ideas and solutions during those walks. Also, I discovered that rather than have self-care take too much time—which was my initial fear—I found that because I was more centered, I actually felt as if I had more time during the day. My work and my personal life became more balanced; I relaxed more, and I gained a new perspective on my hectic schedule. Finally, I had some control over my life!

I still make daily self-care a priority, and it has paid huge dividends in all areas of my life. Emotionally, I'm more centered, and spending dedicated quality time with those who are important to me helps me remember why I'm working so hard. If you find yourself out of balance, or if you feel you just don't seem to have the time to do the things you want to, then make an effort to identify the daily self-care items that will nourish you and give you balance throughout your day. Not only will you feel better about yourself, but those around you will appreciate the more relaxed and present-centered person you've become.

84

View your problems as solutions in training.

L et's face it: life is always going to throw problems, challenges, and situations your way that you're either not prepared for or that you don't want. It's been that way for as long as I can remember, and so far, it hasn't changed. In fact, just when I think I have everything under control, or just the way I like it, something unexpected pops up that I must deal with or fix. I'm sure your experience has been similar. While we all have to deal with problems, though, what is vastly different is how we handle them. Some people seem to have been given an owner's manual to life and so seem to know intuitively how to handle life's problems, whereas others can become flustered or can begin to obsess and worry over them. Now, it's true that some problems are worse than others and, it might be argued, worthy of a little worry. However, once we shift how we look at problems in general, we'll see that we can find better ways of dealing with and eventually solving them.

The first thing to remind ourselves when an unexpected problem or situation comes up is that while we may not have anticipated a particular problem, chances were good that something was going to require our attention at some point. In other words, the universe isn't picking on us. That may sound strange, but it's natural to feel a little self-pity when something doesn't go our way or feel frustrated or even angry if we think that we're being singled out. "Something always has to happen to me!" is a common form of self-talk. Truth is, though, you aren't being singled out; rather, it just happens to be your turn. Learning not to take problems or unwanted situations personally is the first step to accepting them and to freeing you up to find a solution to them.

The other important thing to focus on when a problem comes up is to remember that whatever it is, it's temporary. It's easy to lose this perspective when we're in the middle of a problem or when something happens. Once we remind ourselves that this, too, shall pass, it allows us some space to deal with it in a calmer way. Knowing that whatever is happening right now isn't going to be something that we'll have to deal with forever takes much of the fear and dread out of it and allows us to search out a solution to it. That's the next important thing to remember: whatever it is you're dealing with, there is a solution to it. You may not know what that solution is right now, or you may not like what you think it is, but just like all other problems you've had to deal with (the vast majority, by the way, which you don't even remember), this one, too, has a solution, and you'll find it. Perhaps a friend or family member or neighbor has had a similar problem. If so, then remember it's always easier to leverage someone else's experience rather than figure it out on your own. In fact, sharing your problem with another is one of the best ways of getting support and not feeling so alone with it. The saying "A problem shared is a problem halved" is very true.

By accepting that problems are a normal part of life, that they are almost always temporary, and that there are solutions out there for them, we can begin to see problems for what they are: solutions in training. By looking at problems in this way, we can focus on finding those solutions and learn to appreciate the growth that comes with them. Moreover, adopting this attitude allows us to maintain a calmer and more centered attitude the next time something comes up—which it inevitably will.

85

Create space in your life.

I once heard it said that if you want to know the state of someone's consciousness, all you had to do was look at the state of their closet (or garage). Our physical spaces are often a reflection of our mental spaces, and when they get crowded, ignored, or blocked, it's often an indication that our thinking is overloaded as well. It's like a computer that gets filled up with temporary files and so slows down. Every now and then, it's important to clear these files out, thereby freeing space for the computer to operate faster and more efficiently. It works for our lives as well. Over time we accumulate a lot of stuff—just look into any kitchen "junk" drawer, and you'll know what I mean. By taking some time to clear out that drawer or closet or garage, you'll be creating space and freeing up the corresponding mental energy that will enable you to live a lighter and less stressful life.

Some of you may be familiar with the work of Marie Kondo. She has written books and produced shows on the value of decluttering and letting go of items that no longer serve us. It's interesting to watch one of her episodes when she goes into a home and helps both the parents and kids clear their spaces and organize all their belongings, including giving away objects that no longer "spark joy," as she calls it. As they go through and declutter, organize, and create space in a room or closet, I actually feel myself breathe easier, and once they're done, I feel lighter and more peaceful. While she has since admitted it's hard to adhere perfectly to keeping a spotless house now that she's had kids herself, her concepts of organizing spaces and letting go of excess items, and so creating more space and peace, are still valuable. Decluttering and cleaning a room or home has the powerful effect of freeing you up to live in greater harmony within that space, allowing you to feel happiness with your environment. We all know the feeling we get once our house is cleaned and organized, and that feeling influences the way we think and even our moods. In a sense, we are freeing up the energy that was trapped in the disorganization of the stuff in our lives.

Feng shui is an ancient Chinese practice that optimizes the flow of energy to harmonize people with their environment and with the objects and the space around them. The philosophy teaches that everything both animate and inanimate has energy, and properly directing the flow of the "cosmic current" or energy force, called Qi (spelled "chi" sometimes), can improve wealth, happiness, and even a long life. You don't have to believe in the entire philosophy of feng shui to feel its effect. Have you ever walked into a building or room and immediately felt uncomfortable or cramped? Some spaces just seem blocked or even claustrophobic while in others you feel more relaxed and comfortable. Decluttering your home or car or office has the same effect of freeing the energy that may be trapped and stagnant. Donating items that no longer serve their usefulness or no longer represent the person you are now is also a great way to release energy and create space in your life. The more room you create in your outer environment, the more your inner consciousness clears up as well.

Take some time to look at the areas in your physical space—including your car, office, and even gym bag—that are crowded or blocked. Dedicate some time to cleaning, decluttering, and organizing these areas of your life. Doing so will create space in your consciousness for more peace and happiness to flow into, and soon you'll find yourself functioning a lot more smoothly.

86

You're never too old to start something new.

There is a tendency for many people to settle in their lives and think the window of opportunity to try something new or different or to become something else has shut behind them. Once they settle into their jobs and careers or get comfortable in their homes, neighborhoods, and cities, they tend to dismiss the idea of exploring a new path or pursuing dreams they had when they were younger. "I'm too old for that" is a common refrain, or "I don't have enough _____." I'm sure you can fill in the blank with your own perceived limitations. I read a quote by Nido Qubein (an accomplished speaker and businessman, as well as the president of High Point University in North Carolina) the other day that reminded me of a different way of looking at things: "Your present circumstances don't determine where you can go; they merely determine where you start."

Earlier in the book, I introduced this idea with Ray Kroc's story (the founder of McDonald's). It's important to keep these kinds of stories in mind to help us remember that where we are now doesn't have to be the place we end up later. Years ago, I read about a woman named Edith Murway-Traina. She is a record-breaking weightlifter who holds the Guinness World Record for the oldest competitive weightlifter. She turned 100 recently, and that in itself is a story. She inspired me with the fact that she didn't begin powerlifting until she was 91 years old! I think about her some days when I debate whether to keep going to the gym or canceling my membership and taking up walking. (I still have my membership!)

Another story that inspires me involves the famous golfer Ben Hogan. When Ben retired, he had sixty-four professional victories and nine major titles. He's considered by Tiger Woods and Jack Nicklaus as the best ball-striker the game has ever seen. To hear his story, though, you'd never think he'd end up this way.

Ben's childhood was marred by his father's death by suicide when Ben was just nine years old. He retreated into the solitary world of golf and played incessantly; however, he failed to make the professional tour and was forced to get a full-time job instead. A few years later, he tried the circuit again and made it—yet it was eleven years before his first professional win. Then World War II came, and Ben joined the Army Air Corps while other golfers stayed home and played and improved. After the war, Ben headed back to the tour and tried to make up for lost time. One night, while out driving with his wife, a bus hit his car head on, sending the engine into the driver's seat and the steering wheel into the back seat. He only survived the crash because he dove onto his wife's lap to protect her. Doctors said he'd never walk again, let alone play golf. No one thought that at his age he could start over. That is, no one but Ben. He did walk again, and he threw himself into something that professionals didn't do in those days: he practiced. Ben is credited today as being the first professional golfer to actually practice the game of golf, and he did so relentlessly to regain the use of his body and to relearn the game of golf. It worked, and today, Ben Hogan is one of the greatest golfers in history.

Ben's story is just one of the hundreds of amazing stories of courage and inspiration you'll find in books like Dan Green's *Finish Strong*. I keep books and articles like these all over the house and refer to them often to keep the idea of what's possible—at any age— around me, to motivate and inspire me. I suggest you find stories that inspire you, too. No matter where you are in your life or what your present circumstances are, just remember: they don't determine where you go, only where you begin.

87

You can't change the wind, but you can adjust your sails.

The unexpected situations and problems in life sometimes mimic a coming storm. There can be long periods of calm, where things are going smoothly, but then, out of the blue, something changes, and the wind starts to blow. It may begin with a soft rustling of the leaves in the trees, or quite suddenly the branches themselves can begin to bend and bob up and down, whipping from side to side. Sometimes, the trees themselves can sway and even become uprooted. After the storm blows by, there can be wreckage to deal with and clean away, and sometimes repairs have to be made, and some things may have changed altogether. Life, like the wind, is unpredictable as well; some days your job or your relationship is going smoothly until something changes—little comments you make begin to offend your spouse, or you arrive at work one day to find that your position has been eliminated, and in blows a storm. You never know when things will change, nor can you control them. There is something you can do, however: adjust your sails.

Remembering this can be hard to do, though. We often get locked into a vision for how our lives—and the lives of those we love—should go. We save for college for our kids, but then they decide to take a year off—or not go at all, and the storm is here. Determining what we do next dictates how much peace and contentment we have in our lives.

In the past, I spent a lot of time and wasted a lot of energy being upset when things changed. Whether I had to delay the start of grad school, cut short a vacation I was on, or a client I was counting on canceled, I'd rail against the wind and generally made myself and those around me uncomfortable. By remaining rigid or self-righteous, I was like a branch that is unable to sway and give in to the wind. Sometimes I snapped and occasionally even broke down, causing a scene and unwanted consequences. When I learned to adjust my sails instead—for example, learning to ask, "Is that a bad thing?"—a sense of peace and serenity became available to me, and my life became smoother. The wind no longer blew in my face; rather, it was at my back, and life became easier to deal with (and so was I). I always had the ability, the choice, to do this, and as I began making the right choice, I gained some control over the effects of the weather. By remembering to adjust the sails of myself—my reactions, my attitudes, and my actions—I got to choose how happy I wanted to be.

Being able to go with the flow in this way is a valuable coping skill to develop as we go through the constantly changing weather of life. It starts by checking our expectations as soon as the wind starts blowing. If, when the weather kicks up, we find ourselves getting tense or upset, the first thing to ask is, what did we expect? The moment we identify our expectations, we can begin to release our preconceived ideas and plans and remind ourselves that the wind is the wind—people and events have a momentum of their own, and we can rarely anticipate, let alone, control them. The best course for us to set is to adjust our sails and steer to the nearest safe harbor, given how the wind is blowing at the time. Asking ourselves, "Who could

I reach out to who might have experience with this?" can be a great place to start. By remaining flexible in this way, we can avoid snapping and creating emotional wreckage that we'll have to deal with later. By constantly reminding ourselves that life will rarely remain calm and that situations will always change, we'll be much quicker to adjust our sails to them. Our rides through life will be much more enjoyable for us and all those on the boat with us the sooner we get better at doing this.

First, we form habits, then they form us.

Humans are one of the most adaptive species on the planet. We're quick learners, and we master tasks by developing habits to replace the time and energy it takes to keep learning something over and over again. Think of learning to drive a car. It was awkward at first, and when you took your driver's test with the instructor, you were probably nervous and drove with both hands firmly on the wheel in the "ten and two" position. How about now, though? Most likely, you're on automatic pilot when you drive, and what used to take a lot of energy and thought has become a habit. It's this way with just about everything: Once we learn something, it becomes a habit. We no longer think about or question it, we just do it.

While this is an incredibly useful skill to have, it also has a downside. Oftentimes, the habits we form quickly become automatic ways for us to do something—regardless of whether they are the best way to do something or even whether they are good for us. Just think about your habits of eating or exercising, or how you routinely communicate with your spouse and others in your life. We rarely think of all these habits (and hundreds more); rather, we usually act unconsciously whenever we're given a cue for a response. Eating is a great example. Many people mindlessly reach for a piece of chocolate or other sweet after a meal or when they are hungry. It's just a habit. Others have routine ways of reacting to stress: some people grow angry and act out when set off while others shut down and withdraw. We act on these and other habits without thinking about them, and they soon form our behavior long after we formed them. It just becomes "like us" to act in certain ways. For instance, "It's always like Bob to sit in the corner at a party while everyone else is mingling and having fun."

The good news is that we are still very adaptable, we're still quick learners, and we can change our habits if we don't feel they are giving us the results we want in our lives. Once we form newer, healthier habits, they will, in turn, form a new us as well.

There are a few proven ways to change a habit, and these work with whatever behavior you'd like to improve.

- The first step is to identify a habit that doesn't serve you now. Don't overwhelm yourself at first; instead, pick an easy one you'd like to change—like reaching for a sweet after a meal.

- Next, identify the trigger that sets off this automatic behavior or craving; in this case, it may be each time you finish a meal or when you are bored.

- Once you're aware of the cue, the next step is to have a positive replacement in place for the next time you're tempted. Identifying the replacement in advance and having it ready is crucial to changing a habit. Perhaps a yummy piece of fruit or a piece of your favorite chewing gum works for you. Keep this on your table or desk, and immediately reach for it after your meal.

- Finally, set up a reward for each time you indulge in the new habit. Perhaps place a mark on a calendar or piece of paper to keep track of and reinforce this. You can pick something that speaks to you.
- The key formula is identifying, replacing, and reinforcing.

Given that habits drive so much of our behavior and form much of who we become, it makes a lot of sense to create a habit (pun intended) to review those that are serving you and those that aren't. Think of those you'd like to change and have their replacements nearby. By adopting new ones—consider all those gym-goers who automatically dress for and go to the gym regularly—you'll develop behaviors that will significantly change the outcomes and experience in each area of your life. Remember, once you form a habit, it will form you—for better or worse.

89

Every relationship you have will end one day.

I'll never forget the day my best friend told me this. We were out for our weekly dinner together, catching up on our latest news and progress on various things. I don't know how it came up, but she said something that shocked me at the time. She said that every relationship I had would end someday. She saw my look of disbelief and explained that my parents would pass one day, so those relationships would end, and some friends or people I knew would move away or we wouldn't be as close, and those relationships would come to an end, too. I quickly told her that we would always be friends, and she reminded me that one day one of us would also pass and that our relationship would end as well. It was a lot to take in over dinner, and I don't know why I hadn't thought of it before, but she was right. As I drove home that night, I considered the implications of what she said.

When I got home, my beloved cat, Starlite, greeted me, tail up, meowing, happy to see me. I immediately realized that this relationship was temporary as well. If I needed evidence of this, I had only to think of previous pets I had owned. All were beautiful, nourishing relationships and in the end, temporary, as my friend had suggested. As I went through my week, I realized that everyone I interacted with—neighbors, work associates, close friends, and family—all these would end at some point in the future as well. These relationships were finite, not infinite as I had vaguely imagined them to be. As soon as I made that connection, I realized how precious they all were. There was a finite amount of time I had to spend with each person in my life, and it was up to me to both enjoy that time, and to add as much meaning to it as I could.

As I changed my perspective in this way, my attitudes and actions automatically changed as well. I became more patient around people, and being kinder and more understanding became my default. Suddenly, the small things I used to blow out of proportion or nitpick about faded away as I took a deeper view of what I came to understand as our limited time together. Whether it was just interactions with strangers at the airport or market or with friends and family members, I realized that each interaction was indeed precious. Once I held them in this light, I was able to be more present in them and so get more out of them.

Soon, I made the logical leap and realized my relationship to all things was temporary as well. While I technically owned my home, for example, in reality I was just staying in it for a while. All my furniture, clothes, etc., were only mine temporarily, and this realization created a new appreciation for them. What started as a shocking revelation turned into an awakening for me. Everything I had, including each moment I lived through, was fleeting, yes, but it was also incredibly special. When I began viewing life in this way, I became grateful on a level I can barely explain. I don't always stay on this level, to be sure; however, I now have great awareness of it, and when I surrender to it, I see life for the miracle it is.

Many of us go through life as if it were one big obligation: work, kids, chores, in-laws, family, and more. Once we see all these interactions as they truly are, however—as limited opportunities to impact someone, to love them and make a real difference in their lives— then these same interactions are transformed. Look around you right now. Everything you see, everyone you know, even the earth itself will one day be gone. The time you have now, the opportunities you have to share joy, and your ability to deeply appreciate the miracle of life around you exist in *this* moment. Every relationship you have is priceless: make sure to enjoy them to the fullest.

90

Feelings are not facts.

eelings can take us on a roller-coaster ride. Being anxious is a good example. Sometimes, an impending event or imagined outcome will cause us to be fearful, to worry, and soon we'll become increasingly anxious over how it might turn out. Constant anxiety like this can become debilitating, and while we engage in it, our feelings can turn darker and darker. After everything is settled, though, we often look back and realize what our feelings put us through was far worse than the actual event itself. As we review what we just went through mentally, many of us know what an emotional hangover feels like, and as new feelings of guilt or regret and even shame descend, we can beat ourselves up over them.

What many of us fail to realize, however, is that feelings are not facts—they're just feelings. Even though they seem real enough at the time, in truth, they remain just our thoughts. The pictures they paint aren't happening in the outside world—only in the theater of our minds. When we can step back and see them for what they are, temporary emotional states, we can learn to sit with them and realize that feelings, in themselves, won't hurt us. Most importantly, feelings will pass and change if we give them enough time.

The first step to getting a handle on your feelings is to identify you're having one. I know that might sound strange, yet some people can get so wrapped up in them, so identified with them, that once a strong feeling kicks in, it's as though they jump on a roller coaster. The door snaps shut, the bar descends, and the ride takes off. Once you realize you're on the ride of a strong emotion, though, it's important to just sit with that feeling. It even helps to say to yourself, "I'm having a strong or uncomfortable feeling right now. I'm feeling anxious about my upcoming appointment." Just identifying and naming an emotion helps you disconnect from it. Suddenly, the feeling isn't *you*; rather, it's just an emotional state that's happening in your head. Once you get some distance from it, you realize the second truth: this ride is going to end.

I like to think of feelings as clouds in the sky. When you look at clouds, you notice something interesting about them. At first, clouds seem to be stationary; they are just there. But if you pick one out and stare at it, you'll notice it's actually moving. In a half hour or so, it's not overhead anymore, and often the blue sky and sun appear. Feelings are like this, too. If they are dark or heavy, they seem to sit above you and weigh you down. Once you identify them and stare at them for a while, you'll realize they are constantly shifting, changing, and moving on. When you learn to just sit with and observe your feelings, you'll develop the amazing ability to detach from them and watch them pass you by. This is the beginning of freedom from your feelings.

Once you gain this freedom, you'll discover the other truth about them: they aren't facts after all, they're just feelings. We all have them, all the time, and many times they pass by without causing a disturbance. The next time they do, think of them as a roller coaster inviting you to come for a ride. Consciously decide not to get on, and instead, tell yourself you'll sit this one out this time. Then watch as it takes off, goes up and down, and listen to the screams of the riders. Aren't you glad you didn't get on it? Remember that you always have the choice to take that ride or not.

91

Practice mindfulness.

Earlier in this book, we learned about the immense benefits you can get from developing a meditation practice. If you tried it and found it difficult to sit still and calm your mind, you needn't stress about it. Fortunately, there are other ways to meditate that you can do during your daily activities and ways you can still reap the enormous benefits you'll receive from slowing the mind down, becoming present, and cultivating a space where peace and serenity can enter your life. This type of meditation is called practicing mindfulness, and it's easy and fun to do. You simply focus on becoming intensely aware of what you are doing, feeling, or experiencing in the present moment—without interpretation or judgment. There are many ways of practicing mindfulness, and here are three of my favorites.

Mindful breathing. This first technique is perhaps the most valuable because it can be practiced anytime and anywhere. I practice this when I'm driving or standing in line somewhere and even while I'm working. Mindful breathing simply involves consciously drawing your attention to your breathing and slowing it down. To try it now: Bring your attention to your next inhalation, and then slowly and completely breath that out. Next, breath in slowly and consciously, noticing how it feels in your nose, lungs, diaphragm, and so forth. Do this for a few minutes, deepening your breathing and concentrating solely on the act of breathing. Your only goal here is to become aware of this simple act that you perform automatically thousands of times each day.

Concentration. Someone once said that anything is interesting if you stare at it for a few minutes. To try this, pick up something now—an item on your desk or table, a flower, or just look down at the fabric on your chair or couch—and really look at it. Imagine it is the first time you've seen it and become mesmerized by it. Take in its texture, temperature, color, and simply observe it with a quiet mind. Practice this without interpretation, association, or judgment. Just become deeply aware of its complexity, its uniqueness, its presence. As you do, notice how your mind calms down, how the very act of concentrating brings thoughts to a standstill. This is meditation.

Walking meditation. This is my favorite way of practicing mindfulness, and you can engage in this kind of meditation anytime you are walking—from your car to your office door or the post office or any other store. The key here, again, is to focus intensely on the activity itself. Simply draw your attention to each step you take, one leg at a time, and bring your awareness to your breathing as you walk. Purposefully feel your leg muscles, your feet as they touch the ground, and notice your arm movement and your head position. Quiet your mind and think of nothing except the step you're taking. If you have a little time, try slowing your pace down and moving purposefully, mindfully. Walking meditation is great because you can practice it anytime you have to walk somewhere, anywhere at all. I love walking to the mailbox each day, and I slowly walk up and back our long driveway, intensely aware of each step. I consider it a mini-meditation each day, and I look forward to the calm and peace I get in the middle of each afternoon.

As you can see, there are plenty of opportunities in your everyday life to slow down, become more present, and practice mindfulness. You can search the Internet for articles on different techniques and practices (awareness of your body and releasing tension are great ways as well), and I encourage you to find some that resonate with you. Once you try them, you'll find the benefit of mindfulness is always available to you. Even right now.

92

That's fine, but what would you do if you wanted to be helpful?

L ife doesn't always go the way we want it to. From simple annoyances like waiting on hold too long to bigger inconveniences such as canceled flights or responsibilities at work being shifted to our department or from another team member can upset our plans, making us frustrated or even resentful. If we let these feelings dictate our reactions, it's easy to blow them out of proportion. We can quickly become part of the problem—treating others poorly, snapping at a loved one, becoming spiteful toward our bosses or coworkers; I'm sure you could add to the list. Escalating small problems like these can quickly make our lives unmanageable (others', too!) and can color our attitudes for days—or even weeks. Thankfully, there is another way of handling them.

Knowing these kinds of inconveniences happen all the time and taking a different approach to these situations can dramatically change both our reactions to them and the emotional fallout they can lead to. The first part of this saying, "That's fine," helps us accept an event or situation for what it is—usually something we cannot change. Next, by focusing on a different reaction, in this case "being helpful," we're able to shift our attitude to contributing to a solution rather than adding to the problem. When the customer service rep comes on the phone, we can practice being polite rather than impatient, or in the case of a change in travel plans, we might remember the attitude "Is that a bad thing?" and look for new and better opportunities. At work, there are many ways to contribute and be supportive, and all our coworkers will be thankful for the extra help.

Changing our reactions to these and other situations has other benefits as well. When we look for opportunities to be helpful, we become more cooperative, easier to get along with, and we foster feelings of gratitude from others. Our sense of self builds from feelings like this, and soon the inconvenience fades, and we often carry our positive, helpful feelings into our next interaction. Carefully tending to our attitudes and cultivating a helpful response greatly affects our moods and the moods of others around us. By doing this, we soon see opportunities to be helpful everywhere: at the market, at parties, with family, or at work. Let's face it—life will still be filled with inconveniences and disappointments, and that's fine. Looking for how we can help make things better will always improve both the situation and ourselves.

93

"Trust yourself. Be militantly on your own side."

—Anne Lamott

When you think about the characteristics of great leaders, the great innovative thinkers or inventors, whether in business or science or medicine, or any field, it's easy to identify the qualities that drive them: vision, tenacity, determination, and perseverance, among others. The one that stands out the most to me is that they all had an unwavering belief in themselves and in their ability to bring about their vision, no matter what the current circumstances were like or what others thought. Their ability to trust themselves, to rely on that inner voice—the intuition we all possess but sometimes don't listen to—is what these leaders depended on to the exclusion of all else. Where did the courage and conviction to listen to that voice come from? Were they just born with it? Or did they develop it, and if so, how can we learn to trust ours more?

These were some of the questions that intrigued me when I transitioned to business coaching and training all those years ago. What made some business owners and sales teams better than others? Why did some people perform at the top while others—who had the same training and resources—struggle to produce results? After studying, coaching, and achieving top performance myself, I discovered what it was: absolute trust and belief in yourself. The kind of belief that tells you that you will succeed no matter what; that everything you need to accomplish any internal vision you have is out there somewhere, and you'll find it. I once read that Napoleon said, "The improbable we'll do at once; the impossible might take a little longer." It is this ability to be militantly on your own side that makes the difference.

Some people are born with a more developed sense of belief in themselves than others. My wife is a good example of this. She relies on and trusts in her initial feelings, her intuitions, and as such, she's strong, confident, and self-assured. I wasn't this way earlier in my life; I was hesitant, doubtful, and I had trouble making up my mind. What changed for me was not only recognizing my ability to work hard and persevere, but more importantly, I started listening to and trusting in my inner voice—my intuition. We all have access to that voice, and it speaks to us constantly, and learning how to tune into it, to follow its wisdom, can change your life.

The best way to start is by getting quiet and asking yourself for your inner answer whenever faced with a decision. It's important to tune out all the noise around you, the conflicting opinions and advice of others, and give yourself the space to hear what your intuition is telling you. Don't be pushed into making a decision when you're not ready to (refer back to the earlier quote "You've given me a lot to think about. Let me get back with you."); instead, give yourself some time to let your feelings speak to you. You can tell the difference between your authentic inner voice versus the unhelpful chatter by paying attention to what gently comes up again and again—those thoughts that really resonate with you. They may be quiet at first; however, they will always reveal themselves to you if you give them the time and space to do so.

Relying on your intuition is like exercising a muscle: the more you do it, the stronger it gets. If you're not used to listening to it or following its quiet voice, then give it time, and keep referring to it. Try it with all the decisions you have in a day, especially the easy ones, like what color you'd like something in, and listen to its response. By continuing to do this, it will reward you with the knowledge and decisions that are right for you. Your truth is always available to you, it is uniquely yours, and it is always militantly on your side. Trust it, go with it, and express the vision it offers you. To do so is to become the leader of your life.

The most spiritual thing you can do is to help someone.

Many of us engage in a spiritual path to feel more peaceful, more content, and happier in our lives. We also, however, spend a tremendous amount of time and energy pursuing other things we're convinced will give us these same feelings. We work hard at our jobs to earn enough money to buy material items that give us a temporary feeling of happiness, like new clothes or jewelry, expensive cars, gourmet meals out, or a big house. We pursue relationships we think will complete us, and we engage in many other activities as we chase feelings of contentment: hobbies, travel, spending money, saving money, finding the right career, and on and on.

Those of us who do attain some of these things often discover they don't give us the lasting feelings we thought they would. When we do get them, we find that the sense of happiness they give us is fleeting or not as satisfying as we hoped it would be. Even the job or career that we are sure will validate us can sometimes wake us up in the middle of the night and haunt us with feelings of emptiness. The vacation we looked forward to? Halfway through it, we're already thinking about coming home to our routines, or planning a bigger, better one that will finally give us the joy we're sure awaits us at the next destination.

Peace, contentment, happiness: when we try to acquire these things outside ourselves, we set ourselves up for failure. There is nothing that we can add to our lives that will give us these feelings permanently, deeply. That's because it's a spiritual axiom that to truly get something, you have to give it away. The way you receive love, for example, is by giving it away. The way you acquire meaning in your life is by adding meaning to another's. The power of this simple fact is that you can test it easily and get immediate confirmation of its profound truth.

I have an elderly neighbor across the street. She's in her eighties, and a year ago, her husband passed away. Her driveway is at a sharp angle, and I sometimes see her waddling cautiously down to her mailbox. Lately, when I see her empty garbage and recycling bins on her curb, I'll walk over and haul them back up her driveway next to her garage. I don't do this for acknowledgment, nor am I seen by her or other neighbors. I do this because when I walk back to my house, I have a deep feeling of calm and contentment—a lot more than I get from the Amazon truck that delivers the next package.

This feeling I get from helping another is available to all of us, all the time. It can be as simple as holding the door open for someone, giving a shopping cart to someone in back of us at the market, or calling a friend or family member and asking them how they are. Spirituality and feelings of peace and contentment are found in the act of giving, never in getting. We all have the capacity to give, and so we all have the immediate ability to feel the peace we long for. Once you recognize this, you'll see that you don't need to add any outside things to your life to feel better. You just need to give more of yourself away. And you can start doing that right now.

95

Use your self-talk to build yourself up instead of tearing yourself down.

D o you talk to yourself? At this moment, some of you may be thinking, *Talk to myself? What do you mean talk to myself? I'm not a crazy person!* And, of course, you'd be talking to yourself. The truth is, we all talk to ourselves, and we do it much more frequently than you'd imagine. In his book *The Voice Within*, Charles Fernyhough, a professor at Durham University in the United Kingdom, cites one researcher who claims the average person speaks to him- or herself at a rate of 4,000 words per minute—ten times faster than we speak verbally! That's a lot of self-talk, and in itself that's a staggering discovery. What's even more important, though, is what we tend to say to ourselves. It turns out that much of our self-talk is judgmental, and even critical, and phrases like *How could I be so stupid?* and *There I go again, what's wrong with me?* often follow mistakes we make or when we do things that embarrass us. While at first, these statements may seem harmless, they have a bigger impact on our self-esteem, our future actions, and our outlook on life than we might think.

It's a sobering thought to consider how others would react if we spoke to them the way we speak to ourselves. Imagine, if when one

265

of your friends or coworkers made a mistake, you said something like "That was the dumbest thing I've ever seen! How could you be so stupid?" You wouldn't have many friends, would you? When we turn that around and realize we regularly speak to ourselves that way, it's no wonder we sometimes have low self-esteem or that we doubt ourselves or don't feel as good as we'd like to. Such negative self-talk can't be good for us; indeed, it's not. Our self-talk not only contributes to how we feel about ourselves, it actually predicts our behavior as well. If we're in the habit of telling ourselves that things are likely to not work out, life can soon become a self-fulfilling prophesy. By adopting a negative mindset about ourselves or about situations we're likely to encounter, we seem to search out trouble and problems, and we usually find them. Then we reinforce it with more negative self-talk: "See? I told you that would happen. Happens every time!"

Becoming aware of your negative self-talk is the first step to intervening and replacing it with more positive statements that can support the feelings and outcomes you'd like to have. Positive self-talk has many more benefits as well, including helping you focus on all sides of an issue instead of just the negative side of things. Because situations are rarely black or white, good or bad, it's important to be able to consider what you learned instead of just what you may have done wrong. Developing positive self-talk is also vital to building a positive self-image and to developing your problem-solving skills. Try telling yourself, for example, that while something may not have gone the way you wanted it to, there are things that you'll do differently next time. You are then more likely to keep trying, to take more risks, and to succeed more of the time. When things work out that next time, you can reinforce this with even more positive self-talk, like, *See? I thought that might work* and *Good for me!*

I'm glad I didn't give up, and next time, I'll even. . . . Building your self-esteem contributes to increasing confidence, and this allows you to feel more in control of the events in your life. Just like negative self-talk can have a downward spiral effect, positive self-talk has a positive overall effect that supports you in setting and achieving more goals.

Positive self-talk also contributes to better relationships with others. When we feel better about ourselves, our outlook on life changes; we begin looking for ways to contribute to situations and to assisting others. We become more caring and supportive in general. By adopting a more positive dialogue with yourself, you'll find that you'll be quicker to support and build up others as well. That's something everyone can feel good about!

96

Would you rather be right, or would you rather be happy?

S ometimes, I'm convinced that I'm right about nearly everything. I laughed out loud when I heard someone say in jest,
"Those people who think they know everything are especially
annoying to those of us who do!" I think many of us also secretly feel
this way, and we are quick to share our opinions and even argue and
defend them in the hopes of changing someone else's mind or having
them eventually break down and acknowledge that we are right. As
you've no doubt experienced, this is not a recipe for happiness. Insisting on being right almost always forces someone else to be wrong—
and that means neither one is going to be happy.

The truth is, we are both right—for us. I once read that you cannot reason a man out of something he was never reasoned into. Most
of the beliefs, attitudes, and views we have were conditioned into us
when we were children. Our parents', grandparents', siblings', teachers', friends', societies', and cultures' beliefs and attitudes have been
hardwired into us before we ever had the ability to reason through
things ourselves. Other people believe in their point of view just as
much as you believe in yours. Trying to reason or argue against this
conditioning is rarely effective. This is one reason there is so much

animosity between religions, political groups, and countries. Once we recognize this, we see that we can be both right and happy.

The way to do this is to replace our desire for being right with a desire for being open and interested in others' viewpoints instead. Recognizing that other people's conditioning, experiences, and attitudes are just as valid for them as yours are for you frees you to be accepting of their unique ways of looking at and interpreting the world—without being threatened and without yours being wrong. Once we put aside our agenda of being right and our mission of convincing others to our point of view, a magical thing happens: we discover the path to peace, and we begin truly getting along with others. Also, by stepping outside of our conditioning, we become receptive to learning something we didn't know and to looking at the world in a different way. This is how we begin reasoning for ourselves, how we grow, and how we adopt a more open attitude toward other people. The next time you meet someone with an opinion or attitude different from yours, remind yourself that they are just as right as you are. It's the quickest path that will lead to happiness for you both.

97

"If you don't get everything you want, think of all the things you don't get that you don't want."

—Oscar Wilde

Whenever I see someone in a wheelchair or similarly disabled, I have a great rush of empathy for them. The next great rush that comes to me is one of slightly shamed gratitude. In that moment, I realize the enormous gifts I have—in this instance, the ability to walk and run and move about in any way I choose. I say "slightly shamed" because most of the time I take these things for granted or as my birthright just because I'm alive.

Many of us can feel entitled to the everyday conveniences we have that, once we stop to think about it, millions of people don't have at all. Fresh drinking water is a good example. This is something we take for granted every day, something that we feel the state or city owes us just because we live there, yet in reality, it's not like that at all. Many of us are immensely fortunate to live in a state, province, or country that allows us access to this basic human commodity. I was watching a show on TV the other night, and the people who lived in the city that was featured didn't have access to fresh water. In fact, they spent every other day hauling receptacles to collect water from a central location, and they waited in lines for hours under the scorching sun.

They then had to haul heavy water containers back to their homes miles away. In addition to this, they still had all the chores you do (perhaps even more as, for some, the electricity was inconsistent, air conditioning was nonexistent, and many family members lived with them). All this inconvenience and effort for something I routinely use and to which I don't give a second thought.

Years ago, I watched another show on children who couldn't walk. They sat in their wheelchairs for the interview and talked about what they missed most, and they all said the same thing: the simple ability to be able to run around and play with the other kids. When I looked at what they were wearing, I saw it was a brand-new, or what looked to be brand-new, pair of tennis shoes. That's when it dawned on me: those were shoes that would never wear out. The soles on those shoes would forever remain new. Once again, I felt slightly guilty for something I not only took for granted but even had the audacity to complain about: how quickly the soles on some of my athletic shoes wore out. In that moment, I gained an appreciation for the gift of being able to wear my shoes out, and each time I examine a pair now and see the wear pattern on them, I think back to those kids unable to run and play. Their only wish is to be able to wear out a pair of sneakers, something most of us do all the time.

There are many other things we all take for granted, take as our right just because we think we deserve it. We complain sometimes that we don't have a better car or job or the newest tech device. In most societies, we are inundated with advertising and commercials designed to sell us stuff. These advertisements often make us feel less than if we don't have the latest or better material item. Too many of us buy into that lie. If we stop to look at the flip side of that and start thinking about all the things we don't have that we don't want—illness is a good example—it's super easy to get what I like to call "right-sized" and remember who I am. I'm one of the very lucky ones in this life. I live in the twenty-first century, a time when the standard of living has never been higher. I happen to live in a country that, even with its struggles, offers freedom of thought and expression, and one that offers opportunities based on effort and ideas and hard work. I'll bet that if you're reading this book, then you, too, have access to much more than you might regularly acknowledge. The truth is, we all have many things to be eternally grateful for, and if and when we forget that, we just have to think of all the things we don't have that we don't want. This always puts it in perspective for me.

98

Learn to live with unresolved problems.

O h, if life would just behave! We work so hard to get it just right, to handle all the problems that come up, to anticipate and head off others, and we're sure that if we could just get past this current situation or inconvenience, then we'll have some peace. Finally, it'll be smooth sailing, and we'll be able to breathe easy, enjoy things, and stop stressing. Unfortunately, it rarely goes that way, or if it does, not for long. Inevitably, something else goes wrong or an issue in an area we thought we had under control crops up, and we have to attend to it again. It reminds me of the Dutch kid who sticks his finger in the dike to stop the water from pouring out. No sooner has he done that than another hole sprouts open, and once he plugs that one, another one opens, and so on.

Even though we all experience this, some people (myself included) like to live thinking it will be different. We labor under the delusion that someday life will go the way we want. This persistent illusion is the underlying cause of much unhappiness and discontent in our lives. Learning to recognize it and develop strategies to handle it, though, frees us up to weather the inevitable bumps life throws at us and can give us the ability to be happy, content even, while we're going through the storm. This is where we begin looking at and combining some of the previous strategies we've discussed throughout this book. The key to having an owner's manual to life is to remember that sometimes we'll need several tools to handle a problem, and that by having them nearby, in our toolkit at all times, we'll be able to restore the perspective we need to handle life more gracefully.

Let's briefly consider some of the tools that will help us deal with life on life's terms:

- The first tool to always keep nearby is to check your expectations. What normally gets us in trouble and upsets the peace we want is expecting life to be different than it is at any given moment. By practicing acceptance of what is, and by remembering that life is unpredictable and that challenges will come, you'll be able to stay calmer when the inevitable problems come up.

- Next, when they do come up, it helps to remember they are almost always temporary and that there is a solution to them. Remember, "This, too, shall pass."

- While you're waiting for those solutions to come, it helps to remember that many of the problems you've had before turned out to be opportunities instead. Get in the habit of asking, "Is that a bad thing?" I'm sure you've found solutions that actually enhanced your life, haven't you?

- Also, remember that when something does come up, think about your options and make a decision, and then take an action toward solving it. Even a little action often relieves a lot of stress and needless worry.

- Don't forget that once you've made that decision, make sure to move your mind off the problem and onto the other areas of your life that are going well. Making a gratitude list at this point helps to restore the sense of perspective that, regardless of what's happening right now, your life is probably still filled with a lot of wonderful things. Remember to list at least twenty-five items.
- If you're still not centered, shift your attention to another person, and ask yourself how you can help them. My experience is that when all else fails, involving myself in someone else's life, especially by being useful and caring, always centers me and reminds me that we're all in this together and that we'll all get through it better if we're there for one another.

Using these kinds of strategies can restore the perspective you'll need to learn to live with unresolved problems. Because none of us can avoid them, the happiest among us have learned to roll with the punches, as they say. Getting good at doing this will become one of the greatest life skills you will ever develop.

99

A mistake is only a mistake when you don't learn from it.

Many of us are afraid of making mistakes. It's as though we feel the whole world is watching and that, somehow, we're supposed to know how to do things perfectly. It didn't used to be this way. When we were kids, mistakes were just a part of figuring something out. We didn't give them a second thought; instead, we just moved on and tried again. Intuitively, we knew that mistakes were a part of learning, and that the more mistakes we made, the faster we learned. By learning to reframe mistakes as learning opportunities, we'll not only take a lot of pressure off ourselves, we'll also develop new skills faster and begin enjoying life more again.

I was first introduced to this concept by a personal development coach named Bob Moawad. According to Bob, the only way we grow and become more effective as people is by expanding our awareness, and the best way to do that is by giving ourselves permission to make mistakes. He says that rather than be embarrassed each time he makes a mistake, he simply says to himself, "I rejoice in my expanded awareness!" By reframing a so-called mistake into an opportunity to learn and grow, he looks forward to making them.

He even makes a game of it, and it goes like this: Each day, he gives himself the room to make five mistakes, and he plays carryover. So, on Monday, if he only makes three mistakes by the end of the day, then on Tuesday, he starts the day with seven opportunities to make mistakes. Throughout each day, he "rejoices in his expanded awareness" each time he makes one. He says that some weeks he wakes up on a Friday with sixteen mistakes to make. His first thought on waking up is "What a great day it's going to be today!"

This strategy of looking at mistakes as the learning opportunities they really are offers us a new freedom and reduces a lot of our stress. By making it okay not to be perfect, not to have all the answers, we become teachable again, and we become more willing to engage in new opportunities and challenges. I'm reminded of the saying, "What would you attempt to do if you knew you couldn't fail?" I like to reframe that as "What would you attempt to do if you knew that failing multiple times before succeeding was perfectly okay?" By recognizing mistakes as opportunities to grow our awareness of what's possible, we gain the courage to try new things, to be excited about life, to become kids again.

This week, give yourself three to five opportunities each day to expand your awareness, and play carryover. Every time you learn something new (i.e., make a mistake), rejoice! Give yourself the permission to learn and grow like you did when you were younger. If you do, you'll relax a lot more, gain courage to try new things, and your awareness of what's possible in your life will grow. As you do, you might just discover the wonder of the world again.

You can only keep what you give away.

I n a way, many of the strategies, philosophies, and tips we've covered in this book have led to today's quote. Strategies such as being there for someone, helping them, and truly listening to and trying to understand their unique view of the world are all geared to help you add meaning to someone else's life. By doing these things, *you* are the one who grows and ends up feeling better about your life and the difference you can make. The technique of sending a heartfelt card or writing a meaningful email or text is a great example of this: the real gift you receive is the feeling you get from affecting someone's life in a positive way. No one will care about what you accomplished in your career or how much money you made, but they all will remember the warm feelings you brought into their lives, and, as we've seen, these are the memories you leave behind.

Someone once said that the greatest gift you get from loving someone is loving someone. What a simple yet profound statement, and isn't it true? This captures the essence of today's saying because what ultimately has meaning in life is the part of it you share freely, openly, and lovingly. Many of us are blessed with a number of friends and acquaintances, and when we look back over our lives, considering the many lives that have intersected with ours, what we remember are the times when those people extended themselves for us: those who gave freely of their time and help. In college, we used to joke that if you wanted to know who your friends were, just tell them you had to pack and move. Those who volunteered to help were the ones you learned you could count on. They were the friends willing to be there for you, to help you when you needed it, even when you didn't ask for it. Years later, they are the ones most likely to still be in your life, or they're the ones you remember most.

At the end of the day, it's not about trying to keep up with the Joneses, and it's not about evening the score with anyone; it's about how you've been able to make someone feel. We all have the experience of how it feels to receive love, to receive those moments of kindness and deep empathy. We all know the immeasurable value of true compassion—the feelings that stay with us to the end. I'm reminded of investor Warren Buffett's story when he asked the question of how you define friendship to a woman who survived Auschwitz. She said her test was "Would they hide me?"

Ultimately, you can only keep what you give away. I'd like to share my favorite prayer with you to close out *The Owner's Manual to Life*. May it bring you as much peace as it has brought me over the years. It's called the Prayer of St. Francis:

> *Lord, make me a channel of thy peace;*
> *that where there is hatred, I may bring love;*
> *that where there is wrong, I may bring the spirit of forgiveness;*
> *that where there is discord, I may bring harmony;*
> *that where there is error, I may bring truth;*
> *that where there is doubt, I may bring faith;*
> *that where there are shadows, I may bring light;*

that where there is sadness, I may bring joy.

Lord, grant that I may seek rather to comfort, than to be comforted;

to understand, than to be understood;

to love, than to be loved.

For it is by self-forgetting that one finds.

It is by forgiving that one is forgiven.

It is by dying that one awakens to Eternal Life.

About the Author

© Carina Gonzalez

Michael Zajaczkowski received his bachelor's degree in psychology from UCLA, and his master's degree in marriage and family therapy from Antioch University, Los Angeles. Using his training and insights from the therapeutic model, he adapted this experience to the business coaching and training environment and currently runs a successful international consulting business. He has lectured throughout the United States and Canada and has clients in a variety of countries, including Norway, Poland, Israel, and more. Michael has worked with hundreds of companies over the years and has coached business owners and upper-level management on how to set and attain both business and personal goals.

Michael and his wife relocated from Los Angeles, California, to Raleigh, North Carolina, where they enjoy a vibrant community of pickleball players and where Michael spends his time writing both fiction and nonfiction.

You can read more about Michael's background, see his upcoming books, and connect with him on his website, michaelzbooks.com.